Memoirs
of *Galina*

Published by Brolga Publishing Pty Ltd
ABN 46 063 962 443
PO Box 12544
A'Beckett St
Melbourne, VIC, 8006
Australia

email: markzocchi@brolgapublishing.com.au

National Library of Australia
Cataloguing-in-Publication data
        Kuchina, Galina, author.
        Memoirs of Galina : Chinese by birth, Russian by tradition,
        Australian by adoption
        ISBN: 9781925367225 (paperback)
        Subjects: Russians--Biography. China--Biography.
        Australia--Biography.
        305.89171094

Printed in Australia
Cover design by Wanissa Somsuphangsri
Typesetting by Tara Wyllie

BE PUBLISHED

Publish through a successful publisher. National distribution, Macmillan
& International distribution to the United Kingdom, North America.
Sales Representation to South East Asia
Email: markzocchi@brolgapublishing.com.au

Memoirs
of *Galina*

The story of a Russian Australian from China

GALINA KUCHINA
Translated by Marina Tolmachev

"Oh memory of the heart, you are stronger than the sorrowful memory of the mind..."

— *P. A. Vyazemsky*

Author's note

The reader can be forgiven for smiling sceptically when I say that I remember myself as a babe in arms. Are these real memories?

I remember my grandmother's dining room, her enormous table and myself being held by my mother. She is standing near the heater, which warmed two rooms. From this vantage point I can observe my family sitting at the table. They appear to be discussing something very important.

This event could be the result of my imagination based on collective family memories, but I definitely and clearly remember myself in my crib, which stood in the room of my aunt Liza. The sun is streaming into the room and I stand in my crib and sway.

My daughter, Marina, used the same crib 20 years later. Judging by the furnishings of the room, I must have been very young, according to photographs – under a year.

Early Life

I was born in the Manchurian province of northeast China in the house of my grandmother, Varvara Mihailovna Antonov.

My father, Ignatii Kallinikovich Volegov, was an officer of the White Army, which fought against the Bolsheviks. After the overturn and disbanding of the Czar's Army, my father managed to reach Siberia where he organised Cossack regiments to continue the fight against the Bolsheviks. He survived the *ledanoi pohod* (the Ice March) and found himself outside his native land with the departing, but heroic, White Army. This tragic retreat of the army, together with other peaceful citizens, was accompanied by exhaustion, cold and sickness

Many years later I would find out that my father had been married before and, during this retreat, lost his wife and two daughters to illness. I also found out that he

Galina and parents

came from a family of Old Believers.

Manchuria, the town, was small and clean with a large and beautiful train station. The station had a detailed map of the railway network painted on the top section of the wall in the main hall. To me, as a small girl, it appeared quite grand and rather fascinating.

Another favourite landmark of mine was the beautiful St. Innokenty Cathedral. Within its grounds was a children's orphanage, a home for the elderly, and accommodation for priests, the choir master, members of the church choir and for other people who had some connection with the church.

Bishop Jonah, who has recently been raised to sainthood, was buried in its grounds. The bishop maintained a good relationship with the Soviet Consulate and through this ensured that the children and old people were given coal for the winter months.

One family, who lived on the church grounds, had a son who had never walked before. After the unexpected death of Bishop Ionah, the boy dreamt that the bishop came to him saying, 'Take my legs, I don't need them anymore. Arise!'. Next morning, the boy walked. This dream was officially registered as a miracle.

I remember a very large and beautiful department store; Dun Chan. Was it really that big and beautiful? It seemed so to me at the time. The Nikitinsky compound had a gorgeous entrance with polished brass handrails in front of the enormous mirror windows. There was a photo studio in the corner part of the foyer and a hotel was located above the store on the second floor. The Vorobiev Gastronom left an indelible impression on me.

Galina with friend, Galia Vorobieva

The aroma of delicious delicacies always aroused the appetite - the hope of getting something tasty from Mama or Babushka always excited me. I remember our visits to the market. I loved to run to the meat stall owned by my uncles. I could have reached them more quickly by circumventing the market but it was much more fun to run through and see all the Chinese stallholders.

In Zarechka, there was a cemetery where my grandfather,

Feodor Maximovich Antonov, was buried. I don't know why this area was called Zarechka (*za* meaning 'over' and *rechka* meaning 'river') because there was never a river there, nor any evidence of a river. The leather factory, where my father worked, was also in Zarechka. After their wedding, my parents lived in a flat on the factory site, however, they spent most of their time at my grandmother's.

In Manchuria, there was a city park where we often walked in the evenings. Music always played there - it was a place for assignations and promenade. I can't be sure if the town of Manchuria was indeed as I describe it, but this is how it appeared to me through all the periods of my life. My parents left for Hailar when I was three years old but would return to Manchuria a few times a year and stay at my grandmother's. My mother would sew, dress me up like a doll and send me there during Advent or Lent. I often travelled the route to my grandmother's alone.

An acquaintance of ours, Tolia Popkov, worked as a conductor on the train. Mama left me in his care for the journey and my grandmother and Aunt Liza met me when I reached Manchuria. I loved visiting my grandmother and these trips always gave me much joy.

For the Feasts of Christmas or Easter, Mama, Papa, the Lupov family, my mother's older sister Alexandra Feodorovna (Aunty Shura), her husband Alexander Vasilievich and their daughter Vera came to Manchuria. My grandmother was very proud to have her family congregate around her. She loved her sons-in-law and would buy them their favourite cigarettes and drinks. She catered for each individual taste. Papa smoked Dubler and Uncle Alexander smoked Antik. She bought Antipas vodka for one and Zhemchug for the other. This is how it was with everything.

Antonov family portrait, taken after immigrating from Russia to China

China was welcoming to the Russian refugees. The Chinese accepted a defeated, exhausted but heroic, White Army with its accompanying civil citizens. Being adaptable, hard working and good business people, the Chinese were ready to establish a common ground with the Russians. By the time the refugees arrived, there was an established infrastructure in place.

On the 16th of August 1897, the Russian Spiritual Mission was established with an official opening ceremony to mark the official start of work on the building of the Chinese Eastern Railway. In keeping with the agreement between the two countries, Russia provided security for future service personnel as well as churches, hospitals, schools and houses for railway workers.

Family home in Hailar, China

My father writes:

The day when we needed to cross the Chinese border was upon us. About six to seven kilometres before reaching the town of Manchuria, there was no more cannon fire. The rifles became quiet. Somewhere there may have been an occasional shot fired but the constant whistle of bullets stopped. Logically, this quietness should have brought with it some relief at the thought that one is still alive, but in fact the opposite happened. It is difficult to explain but there was feeling of wanting to cry or shout. We were not ready at this time to say, 'Forgive me!'. It is difficult to explain what we felt at that time to someone who had not shared a similar experience. To leave one's own land and go into a foreign land, into which we were not invited, was not easy. All the riches of Russia, all that was accumulated by our predecessors, was left to our conquerors. Will we ever see you Russia, in the way you were? We do not know. Each one of us, filled with heavy thoughts, tried to surreptitiously steal a glance into the eyes of the other to gauge his level of suffering.

Many years later, I had the opportunity of meeting the renowned Russian author, V.G. Rasputin in Moscow. He said that he liked my father's book and that some parts had real artistic merit.

Galina and writer V.G. Rasputin

From what I remember, he especially liked my father's description of the actual Ice March. It was a tribute to the poignant retelling of what occurred by a person who was not a professional writer from one who was established in his field.

I answered, 'Am I actually hearing this from you of all people?'

My mother was brought to Manchuria as a young girl. Her family included her father, mother, three brothers and four sisters. They had lived in the Ural town of Miass.

My grandfather, Feodor Maximovish Antonov, was an entrepreneur businessman/merchant. He traded cattle and grain. He built roads between surrounding villages and towns and was well-off, rich even. He had a marvellous two-storey house in the town square. His plans to send all his children to university came to nothing, with only his eldest child managing to finish high school.

The bloody revolution turned the wheel of history for the whole country and for individuals. The family lost land, property and money through leaving Miass. Having reached the station of Lebiaz, they took a freight train to China. The family managed to reach Manchuria, in spite of suffering from typhus during their journey. After all their wealth, their horses, carriages, stock and property, they began life in China in absolute poverty.

I visited Miass during a trip to Russia with my husband in 2000. Everything that my mother, grandmother and godmother told me about life in Miass became for me so clear and understandable. I visited their house and walked along the streets which my mother and her family had walked many years prior. I totally immersed myself into their previous life. I imagined myself as my mother, playing with dolls in the attic of their large merchant mansion. I imagined how they would have pulled me on a sleigh to school in winter after a filling breakfast of buns and *aladii* (pancakes). I imagined how I would have gone into the forest to gather berries and mushrooms. I saw all this as on the palm of my hand.

This visit to Miass opened to me a new world, a world which I had heard so much about from my mother. This previously imaginary world became for me a bright reality. In Hailar and later in Australia, my mother kept all the traditions that she inherited from Miass, her homeland.

The family brought with them two fur coats to Manchuria. One was made of ferret fur and the other of fox. From the sale of these, my grandfather bought several carcasses of beef from an abattoir and dairy products from a peasant's farm. While one of my mother's brothers, Kolia, worked for the railways, her older sister, Shura, my mother and her younger sister, Marussia, sold the meat and milk products, not in a shop, but at a market stall. They did this through summer and winter.

The youngest sister, Liza, went to school. The oldest brother, Diodor, bought cattle for slaughter. Kostia, the youngest brother, who had a talent for languages, travelled to various regions and negotiated with the Mongol and Chinese traders. This is the kind of childhood that was the fate of my family and my dear mother, who in the freezing cold spent days on end standing by her stall, occasionally warming herself at a stall owned by a kind Chinese man. All nine family members lived in one room.

In time, the Antonovs opened a butcher shop. They moved into more comfortable lodgings and the children were able to resume their schooling. They acquired land on which animals could be kept – not just for slaughter but also for farm work. They bought camels and arranged transport. Life became happier. For a long time the dream of eventually returning to their homeland did not leave them but the thought of returning to the Soviet hell was not an option. They settled in Manchuria.

My father's fate was tragic. Unfortunately, I do not know much about his early life. Being a child, and later a young woman, the stories told by my father found their way into my consciousness, whereas war and politics did not interest me - how very sad.

Now, I would have listened and absorbed all the details of his stories. I do, however, remember my father speaking of a forest. I assumed that his parents were foresters. In fact, he came from a very rich family. This was obvious as both he and his sister studied in St. Petersburg and for a peasant to be able to send his children to the capital, he needed to be rich.

In 2000, during my travels throughout Russia, I searched through government archives and found that he was indeed of peasant stock from Perm. He completed technical school and became an ensign in the army. As an officer he was listed as a member of the non-hereditary nobility. He had been wounded.

The Russian Revolution occurred in 1917 and by 1918 the army disbanded. In his writings, 'Memoirs of the Ice March', we find that having reached Siberia; he formed a brigade at the request of the peasantry and heroically fought the Bolsheviks. At the end of the conflict, having been defeated, he found himself in Manchuria, where he fully comprehended the tragedy of all that took place. Much loved Russia was lost forever. Here began the life of an immigrant, full of belittling and difficulties both moral and material.

As a military man now in China, without another profession or a penny to his name, Papa, like all the other migrants, was in a difficult situation. His first job in China was cleaning out pigsties. He then worked in a bakery and after that found himself in a leather factory where he learnt to prepare and colour leather. My parents met during this time. They gently fell in love. My wise grandmother, Varvara Michailovna Antonova, saw my father as a good, honest man and blessed their marriage. A year after they wed, I was born.

The leather factory belonged to the Kataev, Gorbunov and Shmelev families. The Kataevs and Gorbunovs also came from Miass. Mama and Papa lived on the other side of the river from my grandmother's home, near the factory.

After working at the factory for three years and having mastered the trade, Papa, together with Fedor Potapovich Riabkov, opened a shop trading in leather goods. Their initial stock included three pairs of boots and several pairs of shoes. They opened this store in Hailar and gradually the business flourished. They expanded into making leather coats and eventually had a large store which sold many goods, all of which were made on the premises. This naturally necessitated a move from Manchuria to Hailar.

As a child, however, I did not like this first store. To me, it appeared narrow, dark and totally unimpressive. It did not have any toys – no dolls

As previously mentioned, Dun Chan met my taste in stores. According to my mother, I would see one toy, then a second, then a third. I would then say, 'Mama, let's buy the entire shop.' However, I would only ever receive one toy and soon forgot about the others.

I must confess that my love of things has remained with me to this very day. Another time, I was walking past the same store and ran up to my own reflection in one of their large mirrors. I was very disappointed that the 'little girl' did not wish to return my handshake and to make friends.

I was an only child and was told that I brought my parents much joy and happiness. I cannot remember my parents punishing me for anything but my father's authority was paramount. I tried never to disappoint him. He loved me very much and Mama always remained sweet and loving, dedicating her life fully to Papa and me. It was said that I was my father's daughter. Mama seemed neither offended nor jealous and did not try to win my affection and love. She did not try to bribe me with toys or treats but was simply,

Galina, age 6. First day of school.

without heightened emotions, a gentle and loving mother.

Papa was more emotional. He was very loving and sensitive and reacted to jokes. He was also prepared to be the butt of jokes and during, particularly touching times, was able to shed a tear. He was never embarrassed to show his emotions.

Many years later, my daughter Marina wrote about her grandfather:

My grandfather, Ignatii Kallinikovich Volegov, was a White Army officer who died still loyal to his oath: 'For God, the Czar and the Fatherland'. He was also the only person who refused to drink to Stalin at a reception in China, and survived.

He did not justify his choices in life through hate and although he was very much an anti-Communist he retained a love for his country and the people in it. He never joined any organisations which would have harmed the Russian people in Russia, nor did he berate, those who stayed in Russia. He shared her suffering. He did not feel threatened by acknowledging anything positive that may have come from post revolutionary Russia.

In our home criticism of the long-suffering Russian Church, zloradstvie (joy) at the trials inflicted on the Russian people was anathema. It was unnecessary. I remember my grandfather as a man so confident in himself that he could allow himself to cry if something touched him. He was man enough to apologise, even to a child, if he felt it necessary. He was accepting and I could talk to him about everything that mattered, even The Beatles. In Bernard Shaw's play, 'Pygmalion', it is said that a lady is a lady not by the way she behaves, but by the way she is treated.

My grandfather knew how to treat a child with respect and in doing so laid the foundation for the way I have always, though not always successfully, tried to behave.

The children of Hailar experienced never-ending fun in the summer and winter months.

In the winter, we had our very own ice rinks on two rivers. I remember coming home from school, grabbing a quick bite to eat and then running to the ice rinkd to skate before sundown. Papa built up a small snow hill in the backyard and children from the entire street would come to toboggan down the hill. The boys did this while standing on their toboggans but I was a chicken and went down either sitting or on my stomach. What a wonderful time of pure unadulterated childhood joy.

In the summer, we would swim in three large rivers –

usually without adults. The rivers were quiet, shallow and clean. There were bushes along the banks. I loved to bathe, to read and to wash our clothes and then drape them on the bushes. Everything dried quickly and we returned home clean, fresh and having had a great deal of enjoyment from the water, the sand and having spent time in the company of friends. What joy – bathing in the water and playing on the shore.

Although I loved going to the river, I never did learn to swim properly - which brings me to my next story ...

One day, I went to the river to bathe with my cousin Vera. Vera was a very daring girl who was very spoilt by her parents. She did not recognise any limits and was never punished by her parents. She did whatever she wanted. She was older than me by three years and I naturally wanted to play with her and her friends. They were not too willing to include me in their games, however.

Vera always presented me with certain conditions and gave me the most demeaning roles in her games. If we were putting on a show in the backyard, a show where the audience consisted on neighbourhood children, I was always given the role of a silent flower. I was not allowed to say one word. I would start feeling sorry for myself whilst 'on stage' and start crying.

If Vera and her friends decided to play actresses, Vera was always Marlene Dietrich. The other girls would choose roles according to their tastes. I could only become part of the game if I took on the role of a poor actress wearing, in Vera's words, 'a torn beret', who had lost everything. I agreed, if only to be allowed to play with them.

So, on this terrible day, Vera came to take me to the river to bathe. In order to get from one river to another, one needed to pass the first river by walking on the right side of the bridge. No one wanted to walk across the river, on the left side of the bridge, as it was too deep but Vera, however, was fearless and accepted the challenge. Of course, I had to follow her.

Just as I nearly reached the bank, I suddenly fell into a large hole. Luckily, a family friend named Tatiana Andreevna Kataeva happened to be walking along the banks of the river. She heard Vera calling, 'Help!' and rushed over. At first, she grabbed me by my hair and by my dress but I slipped out of her hands. She tried again and again. After what felt like a lifetime, Tatiana finally pulled me out of the water. What did she end up telling my mother?

I came home timidly. My mother told me off for being late. Having changed into dry clothes I lay on the bed with my favourite grandmother, who was visiting us at the time and said to her, 'Babusia, I have drunk so much water.'

My grandmother understood everything and believed that what I said about having nearly drowned was true. She told my mother. Tatiana Andreevna said that she only managed to save me on her third attempt. If she had not managed I would have drowned.

After this, I lost all desire to learn to swim properly. I can stay afloat and can even swim a little. But, should I imagine that under me there is no bottom, I panic.

Galina with her parents, Marina
and Fr. Andrew Katkoff

Ours was a very traditional family. As a child I felt that my heart beat in unison with the events that were being celebrated by the Church as we participated in all the Church Feasts and honoured the traditions that were connected with them.

Great Lent, Passion Week, Confession and Communion – the entire school or class prepared together and shared the experience.

The feelings of reverence and full immersion in the events leading up to the sufferings of Christ, their culmination during the services of Holy Thursday and Good Friday to the joy of hearing the words, 'Christ is Risen!' at the midnight Pascal service. I was really in the moment. I felt that Christ rose, 'Now, at this very moment.' I trembled and a feeling of deep joy filled my child's soul, my eyes were filled with tears and I felt with my heart the presence of the risen Christ. As an adult I miss experiencing this heightened spiritual awareness.

Preparation for Christmas began several weeks before the Feast with the making of *pelmeni* (dumplings). In our small town of Hailar, everyone knew at whose place the *pelmeni* were being made so friends arranged working bees at each other's houses. It became a pleasant but necessary chore.

We children loved these types of working bees. Although we were not actually allowed to make the *pelmeni,* we were allowed to roll out the dough. We were pleased to be allowed to participate and to listen in to the adult conversation.

The finished *pelmeni* were frozen and poured into bags. Enough were made to last until Theophany, the period known as *sviatki.* Even without freezers, in China as in Russia itself, *pelmeni* were kept frozen in the larder. Our storeroom had a large tub lined with a linen bag into which the *pelmeni* were poured. We used to go down with a large scoop or a deep dish and scoop up the *pelmeni* to be boiled and enjoyed.

Now, 40-50 years later, living in Australia, we continue to enjoy *pelmeni* and have introduced them to our Australian friends for whom this simple dish has become a delicacy. Meat and poultry was bought. Various delicacies were prepared – sausages, jellied meats and pates.

Closer to the day, tortes and cakes were baked. Houses were cleaned and decorated. Curtains were taken down and together with tablecloths and napkins were laundered. Given the freezing weather during that time of the year, this was no easy task. Everything was hung out on ropes in the courtyard. All the laundry froze and was brought into the house for the night as it could be stolen. Our home felt cosy, filled with the fresh fragrance of the *fir* (Christmas) tree.

On Christmas Eve, while I was in a deep sleep, the decorated Christmas tree appeared. For a long time I was sure that it was brought by Grandfather Frost, yet even when I was certain that a loving Mama and Papa did all, I preferred to cling to the illusion – still trying to continue the fairytale, still wanting to believe in Grandfather Frost.

Early Christmas morning, young children, usually boys, came to sing carols. The night before, Mama prepared small coins, lollies, nuts and other treats and these gifts were distributed to the various groups of children who came throughout the morning.

From morning, the table was set with festive food – a smorgasbord of savoury delicacies, wines, cakes and sweets. *Viziteri* (visitors comprising husbands and male friends) started arriving around midday. The tradition of entertaining *viziteri* was in all families – rich and poor.

The lady of the house prepared a feast according to her means, but each table reflected the joy of the occasion. The men went from house to house and visited the ladies. The ladies welcomed them and accepted their congratulations on the Feast. The men stayed long enough to toast the special day with a drink followed by a little to eat and would then hurry off to repeat the same at the house of the next lady. By evening there was quite a competition between the ladies as each counted up how many *viziteri* she had throughout the day.

On the first day of Christmas or *Pascha* (Easter), the priest and members of the choir would usually visit each home and conduct a short service culminating in a particularly joyous singing of the Troparion (festive hymn). These wonderful moments will never be forgotten and will continue to warm my heart. I will forever admire how carefully my parents preserved and passed on these traditions.

In the evening on Christmas Day, new, this time older, carol singers came carrying a large paper star of different colours. In the star there burned a candle before a picture of Christ in the manger and the children of the house joined the carollers in the singing of festive hymns and carols. They were also given money and treats.

The second day was the day when ladies made visits to each other. However, these would often end up in one house as many found it difficult to curtail their conversations once they got together over tea. In the evening the ladies were joined by their husbands and the table was set for dinner.

Christmas was celebrated up to the Feast of Theophany (the Baptism of Christ) and Easter up to the Feast of the Ascension, or in some places to Pentecost, also known as Trinity Sunday. So, from the second or third day of

Christmas, the children's parties began.

In each house, rich or poor, there was always a Christmas tree and someone dressed as Grandfather Frost. There were party games and each child received an individual bag from Grandfather Frost. Each bag mostly contained a mandarin, an apple, nuts, lollies and biscuits. Each child had to say a poem before receiving the gift and I remember clearly with what trepidation I approached Grandfather Frost.

The children were dressed in their best clothes and always wore party hats made by the loving hands of their mothers. These Christmas parties were an everyday event right through to Theophany because each mother organised a party for her own child.

As it was winter, apples and mandarins were bought earlier and were kept in the cellar till they were needed. The bags often contained a toy, crackers and sparklers. At sundown each mother would come to collect her child. With Theophany, the partying concluded and normal life began, and for the children – school.

The celebration of the Feast of Our Lord's Theophany (the Baptism of Jesus at the river Jordan by St John the Baptist) was very special.

There were two churches in Hailar. After the Divine Liturgy, there was a procession from these churches to the ice filled river where a cross and an altar table were sculpted out of ice. A festive service in celebration of the Baptism of Christ was served.

During the singing of the Troparion, doves were released.

Young boys would hold the homing pigeons and wait for the words, 'And the Spirit in the form of a dove confirmed the certainty of the Word', to let them go. In his book, 'White Harbin', G.B. Melihov writes, 'From 1921, the blessing of the waters was done on the Sungari river which became for the faithful the river Jordan.

After Divine Liturgy, the clergy and parishioners from all the Harbin churches would go in procession to the river. A font was cut out of the ice and many young bravehearts bathed in the icy baptismal waters.

Many years later, when I lived in Harbin, I always went to the blessing of the waters at the river Sungari. It was very joyful. The procession from the Iversky Church, Sts Peter and Paul Church made its way to the St. Sofia Cathedral.

There, the two groups were joined together into one large procession and made their way to the Blagoveshenski Church (The Church of the Annunciation) where they were joined in turn by the parishioners from the Church of the Prophet Elijah. Here, they met the people from the St. Nicholas Church with banners, singing, the ringing of bells and golden clad icons. The atmosphere was amazing. The reflected sun's rays from the snow and the eight-sided ice cross-created a phenomenal picture.

The sight of such a great mass of people moving along the Chinese streets towards the bank of the river Sungari is impossible to forget. The big joyous flow of people approaches the ice altar.

Even now, Harbin is noted for its magnificent Ice Festival.

Its ice sculptures include an enormous cross, Royal Doors shaped in the form of an arch and decorated with two doves, a candle stand, and a pool-font in the shape of a cross for the believer bathers.

The sacred moment arrives when, singing the Troparion hymn:

When Thou was baptized in the Jordan, O Lord, the worship of the Trinity was made manifest; for the voice of the Father bore witness to Thee, calling Thee His beloved Son. And the Spirit in the form of a dove confirmed the certainty of the word. O Christ our God, Who has appeared and has enlightened the world, glory to Thee.

The priest lowers a cross into the font and blesses the water. The thin layer of ice separating the pool-font is broken and water gushes in. At that moment doves circle the Sungari/Jordan river. Many, including me, bathed in the icy water. Straw was laid around the pool to prevent the wet feet from freezing to the ice. Making the sign of the cross, one lowered oneself into the water three times. There were always people to help bathers emerge from the pool to avoid slipping.

Naturally, one dressed appropriately for this. A towelling robe covered the still wet swimsuit. One needed to somehow take off the swimsuit whilst keeping ones dignity in front of all the people. Then there was the shawl, fur coat and home on a rickshaw. Churches away from the

Sungari river also constructed special 'Jordans', making a small font and erecting an ice cross for the blessing of the waters. Many years later, in 1988, the Lord granted me the opportunity to immerse myself into the river Jordan in the Holy Land.

The flow of people from the Theophany procession interfered with the normal flow of traffic. Because of this, the city transport system changed its timetable. Although there were traffic jams in different parts of the city, order was maintained by the Chinese police who formed a human chain, guarding the Theophany procession for its entire progress.

We left Harbin in 1957 and this tradition continued even after our departure. Many Chinese people also went to the Sungari with buckets and I remember asking one man why he was taking this water home.

'Madam, can't you understand anything. If you drink this water, you will not be sick,' he answered.

I do not remember my parents talking to me about things spiritual – nor did they attempt to impose their opinions onto me – but the picture of family life, the behaviour of my parents, their regular attendance at church, and their performance of rituals and traditions confirmed in me a faith.

A big influence on me and on my spiritual development was Fr. Rostislav Gan. He was our pastor, parish priest and family friend. Again, it was not his sermons, which could not be fully grasped by a child's mind, but the person of the priest, which influenced my view of the world and my spiritual growth.

Easter had a greater meaning for me than the Feast of the Nativity (Christmas), even though Christmas was always considered the 'children's Feast'. We prepared for Easter with Great Lent.

The week before the beginning of Lent, we celebrated *Maslenitsia* (Pancake Week). We enjoyed different types of pancakes, topped with sour cream, sturgeon, caviar, herring, jam etc. Then came Forgiveness Sunday …

On this day, the Sunday Liturgy was always followed by a Vespers service, during which Fr. Rostislav would deliver a strict sermon on the nature of fasting, repentance, forgiveness and reconciliation. The priest would then ask forgiveness from the entire congregation and the members of the congregation would ask forgiveness from each other. There was a general reconciliation within the church and at home amongst members of the family. However, the next day, on the first Monday of Great Lent, the atmosphere completely changes. There are no more dances or concerts. The church takes on a sombre look. The vestments worn by the clergy are now black with white crosses.

During Lent, students go to church for confession and then again to Holy Communion on the following day.

As students, we loved Palm Sunday. We respectfully stood in church in the evening, holding bunches of pussy willow, decorated with paper flowers and candles.

Holy Week was the most difficult week of Great Lent.

Naturally, because of school, we could not attend all the unceasing morning and evening services that were scheduled. However, the services of Holy Thursday, including the Reading of the 12 Gospels as well as the Burial Services on Holy (Good) Friday were never missed. Following the service of the 12 Gospels, people took home the lit candle that they had been holding during the service. They went from room to room and made a sign of the cross on the beam of each door of their house.

Many years later, I was in Moscow in 1992 and by old tradition brought the lit candle to the home where I was staying. This surprised my friends because this tradition had not been followed during Soviet times.

On Good Friday, very emotional services take place – *vinos plashenitsi* (the taking down from the Cross) and *pogrebenie* (the Lamentations). The dimly lit church, with its sombre singing and readings on the Passion of Our Lord, creates a full picture of the tragedy of what occurred. We would return home, with bowed heads, concentrating on the full impact of the sufferings of Christ. But then, *Paskha* arrives ...

The church is brightly lit with chandeliers and candles. The dark coverings and vestments are replaced with white. 'Christ is Risen!' and 'He is Risen Indeed!' echoes through the church. All are joyous, smiling and happy.

I still remember our last Pashal service in the St. Nicholas Cathedral in Harbin. Metropolitan Nestor served as hierarchy of the Moscow Patriarchate. Co-serving were

Bishop Nikandr Leonidov

Bishop Nikandr and a number of priests. I remember how Bishop Nestor, with each cry of 'Christ if Risen!' lifted his hand with candles and we could see all the colours of the rainbow reflected from his crystal rosary beads. This detail has remained with me all these years.

After the service, we went home and broke the fast and in the morning the ladies of the house prepared to receive their *visiteri*.

With the joy of Easter came much work for our mothers especially when they embarked on the sacred duty of baking the *kulichi* (Easter cakes). All the ingredients were prepared earlier. Mama was preoccupied for several days before baking day. Discussions were held with her sister, Alexandra Fedorovna Lupova (with whom they shared a very close friendship). They had to decide whether to bake the kulichi in their own ovens or to take them to the Chinese bakers who provided their ovens for a nominal fee.

I loved the whole preparation process because nuts and

sultanas needed to be sorted. Almonds were covered with hot water to remove the skins; while sultanas were washed to remove dust and sand. Large towels were spread on tables for the sultanas and almonds. How delicious it was to sneak a sultana or almond with Mama pretending not to notice.

The leaven was started at night and from that time to the time that the last kulich was taken out of the oven, women did not have any peace. Concerned faces, eyes full of fear, 'What if the dough does not rise?' So many ingredients could be ruined. So much worry!

Doors were opened and closed quietly. On no account could you bang the door. The dough could sink. Then, the magic moment. The last kulich is taken out of the oven, Mama is glowing, Aunt Shura is happy and everything else – is nothing.

After surviving the baking of the *kulichi*, the tortes, biscuits and other foods are not a problem. The decoration of the cakes and the colouring of the eggs were all a very important part of the preparation and setting of the festive Easter table. Here, the artistry of each housekeeper came to the fore.

Later in Australia, during my long service leave following 25 years work in the hospital, I took a course with Vera Stepanovna Apanaskevich in the special art of cake and *kulichi* decoration. I learned how to make fruit jellies and *zefir* (marshmellow). Unfortunately, calories proved to be a problem. Roses, mushrooms with chocolate tops, flowers etc. made from butter-cream may have looked good but were unhealthy so this art was not used often. However, I did make my daughter's wedding cake when she married Vasia and decorated Christening cakes for my grandchildren.

It is important to describe how *Radonitsa* (remembrance of those who died) was celebrated in Harbin. On the tenth day after *Paskha*, on Tuesday, all Orthodox churches would conduct a general *Panikhida* (Memorial Service). After the *Panikhida* the clergy and people made their way to the Uspensky cemetery where shorter, individual services were held at each grave.

According to old Russian custom, it was usual to bring *kutia* (a bowl of sweetened rice or other grain usually decorated with dried fruit), food and something to drink. People would in this way pray for and remember the departed at the grave site. Special buses were often used and the local authorities ensured that buses, trams and pedestrians all moved in an orderly fashion.

It is sad to note that the Uspensky (Dormition) Cathedral and the cemetery were destroyed during the Cultural Revolution. The memorial stones were then used to pave the streets and the cemetery was razed to become a park. People said that when walking along the streets of Harbin it was sometimes possible to see the names of loved ones and acquaintances among the stones embedded in the paths and roads. These were the grimaces of fate that life presented during the days of 'great changes' which took away and destroyed millions of innocent people in jails, camps and exile.

School & War

I finished school in Hailar at the age of 15. I must have skipped a class at some stage and started school at six rather than the required age of seven. Although I was a reasonable student, I did not put in too much effort or enthusiasm into my studies. Mathematics, algebra, geometry and trigonometry were difficult for me, but, with a bit of luck, I managed to get through them. I loved history and literature, and was immersed in Turgenev, Pushkin and Lermontov. I cried reading about Liza Kalitina and Pushkin's Tatiana.

I sometimes read out loud for hours behind closed doors, or would go for days under the impression of a film or a play. I remember feeling strongly about the film, 'Mary Stuart.' I clearly remember myself as a young girl, walking along the street as a dignified, beautiful though tragic queen, oblivious to the life around me. But, I never wanted to be an actress, in spite of being so dramatically influenced by the theatre. I always wanted to be a doctor. I would set up hospital wards with my dolls as patients and myself as the doctor.

I played with dolls till I was 15 years old. Then, I discovered boys. Prior to this I had many friends who were boys. At school, I shared a desk in the front row, with two boys. My teacher thought that sitting me with the boys would stop me talking in class. She was wrong. Nothing could stop me talking.

I also suffered from an incredible urge to laugh. I was not able to stop myself from dissolving into fits of laughter. I suffered from this very much and my fellow students delighted in making me laugh in class, in church, at school concerts and assemblies, in those places where it is forbidden to laugh. All someone had to do was to lift up a finger with an accompanying facial expression and I'd collapse into fits of unstoppable laughter. Oh, how hard it was for me! My whole body would be engulfed in laughter. I tried everything, physical, mental and spiritual, to try to stop these fits but all in vain. The result was the same, whatever happened, 'Out of class this instant!' Sometimes these words were followed with, 'Once you have finished laughing, you can return to class.'

After making the tremendous effort to stop, and with much suffering, I would at last contain my laughter and return to class. However, upon walking in and seeing the faces of my fellow students, I would remember the funny moment and yet again dissolve into laughter. I would again run out the room, this time *without* needing to be told.

In adulthood I did manage to get rid of this curse, however, in my fifties, it made a reappearance. I was at a violin recital in Sydney when the brother of my girlfriend, sitting to the left of me, began to quietly snore. On the right of me was my girlfriend, looking quite annoyed.

I whispered, 'Leave him. He is tired.'

Her reply was, 'Why is he tired?'

This question was accompanied by such an expression that triggered within me the unstoppable laughter that I suffered from as a child. The hall was quiet, beautiful sounds emanated from the violin and at that very time, I was suffering from a need to laugh, triggered by nothing more than the expression on the face of Masha. Those eyes and that annoyed whisper again destroyed me – a lady who loves music and culture was now reduced to suffering the agonies of trying to suppress a fit of laughter.

It was 1945. The skies over the city prepared for a storm. Dark clouds were forming as more and more Japanese troops were appearing. The railway carried some inexplicable freight to places unknown to us. All those in train carriages travelling from Hailar to Ugonor and from Manchuria to Djelainor were under the strict supervision of the Japanese police. The windows of the carriages were tightly covered with a strong curtain on a spring, held in place by a metallic lock at the bottom of the window. We knew better than to try to presume what was happening outside the windows.

I witnessed an awful scene during one of the train journeys. I was sharing a compartment with a young Japanese girl and her father. She was wearing a school uniform and he was in an ordinary suit. Whether it was plain thoughtlessness or childish curiosity, the girl slightly moved the covering using her finger. I do not know from where, but a uniformed Japanese officer barged in and began shouting at the girl and hitting her across the face. Tears flowed from the eyes of this unhappy child. Her poor father, having bowed his head low, was unable to interfere to help his daughter. I cannot remember what happened after that but the horror of this scene has left an incredible impression on me and even today I shiver when I remember what happened.

During this time, the Japanese (sensing that a storm was brewing) were undergoing serious preparations for war. As school children we had lessons in fighting fires. Windows were blackened out so that no light could escape and lamps in each house needed to have black shades. School uniforms for girls, which usually consisted of a brown dress with an apron, were replaced with trousers and a jacket in camouflage material.

The frightening building which housed the Japanese gendarmes was located close to our school. Somehow, from behind the iron gates, a large dog escaped. Loudly barking and dragging the remnants of its chain, the dog ran towards me and was about to reach me. I ran with fear and horror but at one point realised that it was impossible to run any more.

The dog was upon me and was prepared to tear me to pieces. It already grabbed me by my trousers and as I later noticed, had already ripped off a piece of the material. I stopped and started praying to my Guardian Angel. The dog stopped, turned around and ran back. I believe that my Guardian Angel saved me. A skeptic, however, could say that the dog stopped because I stopped running.

Later, after the Soviet troops entered Manchuria, we found out that in the area between Hailar and the next station, the Japanese were building an underground town with hospitals, dining areas, shops etc. Prisoner coolies who toiled like ants after which the 'civilised' Japanese cruelly and inhumanely killed them did the work. After the war, when this underground space was opened, people continued to die.

When the Japanese were leaving Hailar they placed traps as bait. In one of the underground passageways, they left the body of a Japanese woman wearing a kimono. She wore an *obe* (belt), which held a purse. Under it was a bomb. This is how people died even after the war.

The disappearance of people, their death in Japanese jails and the horrors of these places were only revealed when the Red Army came and survivors were released. Those who were young and had strong constitutions did survive and went on to live productive lives after the war. Some went on to have successful careers, heading up large agricultural enterprises. Older people, however, died within the walls of the Japanese prisons.

The Vorobiev brothers owned a large gourmet grocery store. Both brothers were married. One couple was childless and the other had two children, a daughter Galia, who was my age. She was my friend and had a younger brother – Alesha. When I visited my grandmother in Manchuria we spent most of our time together.

Theirs was a wonderful family. The brothers were always working in the store while Elena Justinovna, Galia's mother and Maria Vasilievna were always home. They were hospitable and nice to us. The house was 'a full chalice', full of abundance. Everyone, young and old, on entering experienced hospitality, warmth, comfort and love upon entering.

They suffered an appalling tragedy. The Japanese arrested both brothers. Elena Justinovna was left broken by grief, dismay and hopelessness and with the responsibility of two children. But Galia did not lose hope. I remember how she came to Hailar. We were both 13 or 14 years old. She decided to intercede for her father and managed to have a meeting with him. She tried to barge into all the doors but it was impossible to get in. Only the optimism and naivety of a child could support the idea that a discussion with the Japanese gendarme was possible. I went with Galia and waited for her outside the gates of the police station.

Fifty years later, in an audio letter from Saratov, Galia thanked me for that support, friendship and faith. She told me about the tragic deaths of her father and uncle. She did not forget that we shared not only her tragedy but also my own fears for my father.

My first question on returning home from school was, 'Is Papa home?' Childhood was overshadowed by the constant fear of arrest.

But no matter what was happening; no matter how we hated the Japanese and their total intrusion into our life, in school we still remained happy, joyful, cheeky children. We began to mature; dolls and other children's games began to lose their charm and were replaced by an interest in boys, dances, music and parties.

We learnt to dance at school and the lessons included the Waltz, the Mazurka, Padekar, Tsiganochka, the Polka, Poka-Babochka and many others. School dances were held in private homes, school concerts were a regular feature of our lives and during summer we often went on picnics with our school friends.

Our lives were full. One activity was replaced by another. I suddenly felt the desire to learn to type and began taking lessons from one of the teachers during my lunch break. Later, this training as a stenographer proved to be an invaluable asset and played a crucial role in my life.

On the 7th of August 1945, my mother and father put me on a train to Hake to spend the remainder of the summer holidays with Aunt Liza and Uncle Dora, who were staying there at the time. I loved Aunt Liza and she loved and spoiled me.

The long summer days were spent swimming in the river, picking berries, and meeting the cows coming back from the pastures. The children went to meet the cows that were making their way directly to the stables in order to be milked. The milk was put through a separator; cream went into the earthenware pitchers and the whey went straight into the buckets for the calves.

Having finished the evening work, girls and boys ran to the meadow for dancing. There was always a person to play the accordion and everyone had plenty of fun. People danced, sang songs and enjoyed themselves. The day involved work in anticipation of the evening festivities. Of course, I was only an observer as I did not have a chance to meet the local youth. Before I had a chance to meet them, the war began

On the 8th of August 1945, Uncle Dora, Aunt Liza and Anya – the daughter of our maid – prepared to go into the fields to pick cherries. All of us were prepared to leave. I remember the cart, the two-harnessed horses; enough provisions for the whole day and of course, baskets for the cherries. Having just settled in the cart we were suddenly overshadowed by the thundering sound of airplanes.

They appeared like a flock of black, loud birds flying

towards Hailar. Memories of the combination of black, loud, frightening 'birds' remains with me for my entire life. The sky darkened and our consciousness dulled. We did not want to believe that this was war. We decided that the Japanese were doing manouvers as we had become psychologically used to them. We assumed that this was a defence exercise and decided to go into the fields as planned.

The day was wonderful. The sun was warm but not so hot that it burned. The bright emerald green fields spread before us and far away, the cherry bushes drew us with the promise of generous crops of fruit. Suddenly, we saw that there were straight lines of marching Japanese soldiers marching along the road. They were in such numbers that the lines appeared never ending. Armed but with faces full of concentration they passed us by without appearing to see us.

After that came the trucks and the tanks. It then became obvious to us that this was indeed war. We needed to return home as soon as possible. The Japanese could have destroyed us with one round from their rifles, but obviously there were no orders issued to destroy civilians during this departure of the army. They were not interested in us and we miraculously survived.

Given there was no radio or telephone, I do not know how the villages already knew that this was war. The people were well aware that the Soviet troops had already entered Hailar and that the Japanese were retreating. The first refugees began to arrive in Hake. Listening to their stories, I became aware of the full horror of what was occurring.

I remember being very flushed because the day was hot and I was worried about my parents. I ran into the courtyard, where there was a large long trough with cold water from the well for the cattle. I put my legs into the trough and, to this day, can feel the effect of the freezing water on my legs.

Having refreshed myself in this way, I ran to the railway station to meet the train carrying refugees. The train had not yet come to a stop but I continued to run, trying keeping up with it. It is still a mystery where I got the strength to do this. I have never been a sporting type of person and this was a truly athletic feat.

The train finally stopped. People began to disembark – all familiar faces. But, where was Mama? Where was Papa?'

I ran along the platform looking for them but they were not there. I was overwhelmed with horror. By now I could hear exploding bombs onto Hailar, flames could be seen from the station of Hake but my mother and father were not there. Suddenly, I saw Fr. Rostislav Gan.

I have already written about him as the priest, whom I respected totally and whose influence on me was strong. He was responsible largely for my spiritual formation because of the respect I had for him and because of the way I was always welcomed into his family.

Fr Rostislav, seeing my distress, told me that he had seen

my parents; he saw that they left Hailar for a safe place and tried to convince me that they were indeed safe. But why were they not in Hake? Why did they not come with the other refugees? They knew that I was in Hake with our relatives.

I wanted to believe Fr. Rostislav, but I was still full of doubt. Traumatised and tired, I returned home.

The refugees left the train station and dispersed around the village, hoping for help from charitable people. Several moved in with us. Among them was a young man. He was a total stranger who, in his own words, was on holiday in Hailar where the war caught him out. He lived in our house for a little over a month as it was impossible to leave for Harbin because the railway connection was cut.

Two years later, and at a ball held at the Harbin, I met this young man face to face. He pretended not to know me. For the first time, I came across ungratefulness.

We all lived in Hake for over a month, cut off from the surrounding world and with no clue about the fate of my parents and other relatives in Harbin and Manchuria.

On the first night of the refugees' arrival, the village population decided to go into the steepe and they feared remaining in their homes. Naturally, I went as well. We walked where our eyes led us and each time we stopped, even if it was for a few minutes, I threw myself on the ground and slept. This was a reaction to the depleted emotions and the body demanded rest.

At last, on reaching a suitable place, we set up camp under

the trees and began to talk about what to do next. The village people were worried not only about themselves but about their cattle. Someone said that several Japanese soldiers entered the village, asked for milk and immediately paid for it with a small piece of soap.

We decided to return home in the morning. Among the refugees from Hailar was Stephan Vinogradoff, the husband of my cousin Vera. His was a very choleric personality. He served in the Japanese army as an officer, although later it was found that he was indeed working for the other side as well. As a person he was fearless, joyous and brave. His work in intelligence deserves another book.

Fr. Rostislav was upset that he did not have a chance to save the sacred vessels that remained on the altar table of his church. Everything happened so quickly. The clouds of planes flew over the city; bullets flew from all directions. The city burned.

Stephan Vinogradoff, seeing the distress of Fr. Rostislav, said to him, 'Don't worry, I will do what I can.'

He somehow managed to obtain a horse and rode to Hailar. He entered the sanctuary, gathered up the tabernacle and all the sacred vessels into the altar table covering and brought the bundle to Fr. Rostislav. We were all amazed at his heroic act in saving these important items from desecration.

I don't remember exactly how long we spent in the steppe. But, having returned home, I totally lost my peace of mind. I suffered, was tortured by my lack of knowledge about what happened to my parents.

Hailar was burning, we saw the fires from our village, we heard the bombing but there was no word at all from my mother and father. I lived with this tension for a month until at last there was a train to Hailar. I was on it. In spite of arguments from my family to stay in Hake, I went home. I needed to find out if I had a home and to find my parents.

Life in China under the Japanese occupation of Manchuria had been filled with an atmosphere of fear. 'Liberation' by the Red Army, whilst bringing an initial feeling of joy at being free of the Japanese, brought with it feelings of trepidation and frustration. What had happened to my parents? Why did I not have any information? Why had no one seen them?

As it happened, my parents decided to join their business partner and try to escape the bombings and fires that besieged the town by taking items from their factory and shop, as well as their livestock, and going into the fields. They knew that I was safe with my relatives and planned, at the first opportunity, to travel to Hake by cart. However, they were unable to do this. Their horses were confiscated and their only option was to return to Hailar.

After a while, the villages returned to their homes in Hake. This was small village, just two or three streets. The houses were not large, either made of wood or clay, with hardened earthenware floors covered by home made rugs. The windows had curtains, there were flowers on the windowsills, pots in the kitchen and the Russian stove dominated most houses. *Palate* (raised sleeping platforms) which were often used by farm workers were in some of the houses.

The Antonov family in China -
Nikolai (Kolia) Antonov, Ignati Volegov, Arkadi Izergin,
Maria Izergina, Aleksandr Lupov, Konstantin Antonov (back)
Kiodor (Dora) Antonov, Antonina Volegova, Varvara Antonova,
Elizaveta (Liza) Antonova, Alexandra (Shura) Lupova (seated)
Galina Kuchina and Vera Lupova (front)

The Antonov family had large sleeping platforms and the refugees used them, a young woman with her nieces and a young man. The owners of the house, my godfather, Uncle Kostia and his wife Aunt Lidia slept in a small room and I, with Aunt Liza slept on the floor in the dining room.

For the Antonov family, the house in Hake was used as a temporary rather than a permanent place of residence as their main dwelling was in the city of Manchuria where they had a large household, another farm and meat storage facilities. But, with the Japanese occupation, life became more complicated and dangerous. People disappeared. Many died in Japanese prisons. Trade and any sort of commercial enterprises were under Japanese control and one did not need to be a criminal or a spy to find oneself in a Japanese prison.

It was enough for a 'caring' neighbour to point you out and your fate was sealed. In order to be less visible, it was decided to move the cattle away from the more central location to Hake, where the family Lupov, my mother's oldest sister, Alexandra Feodorovna and her husband Aleksander Vasilievich with their daughter Vera, lived.

The farm in Hake had large courtyards. There were stables for the cattle, storehouses, and barns for holding farm equipment, a summer kitchen where there was a separator, granaries and a larder for the storage of flour, sugar, dry berries or fresh berries covered by sugar and prepared to be made into jam or dry biscuits. It was usually locked but when Semenova, the maid, who was an excellent cook, went into the larder to get supplies, I did not miss an opportunity to help her and at the same time helped myself to the dried fruit or biscuits.

Farm work continued and returning from the fields there were many duties that still needed to be performed.

After work people talked about the current situation.

On a sunny August day when the first Soviet troops marched into the village, no one actually knew what was happening, but even without a telephone or radio, the news quickly spread. Hearing that the troops were coming, many of us run to meet the conquering army.

The soldiers were marching in columns – peacefully and quietly. We surrounded them as a group and were happy and exhilarated to hear the Russian language spoken. Even though we studied in Russian schools and spoke Russian at home and indeed were immersed in Russian culture at home, it was stunning to hear the Russian language and songs on such a massive scale.

I ran home in an emotional state yelling, 'They are speaking in Russian! They are singing in Russian!' Of course this was the reaction of a young impressionable exalted teenage girl. However, even as an older person, I also experienced pleasant feelings when I found myself immersed in a totally Russian environment when visiting Russia in 1976.

Hearing the cultured voices of our guides was nice, as well as being able to overhear ordinary conversations in theatres, standing in line for coffee and cake or a glass of champagne and sandwich during interval, between two friends or a mother and daughter. Young couples usually did not speak in these situations but simply looked into each other's loving eyes.

I continued to enjoy catching snippets of conversations

in Russia, especially during my early trips to the country. Now, it is sad to hear that so many foreign words have infiltrated the language when there are perfectly good Russian words that can be used instead of the foreign ones. The war caught me on the second day of my arrival in Hake. My parents sent me to the village for the holidays, to breathe some fresh air and to enjoy the joys of village life. I was staying with my closest family, my godfather Uncle Kostia and his wife Aunt Lidia, Uncle Dora and Aunt Liza.

The war surprised all of us. We suspected that something frightening was about to happen because of the heavy atmosphere surrounding the town. Sometimes we saw whole battalions of Japanese travelling into unknown to us directions. Suddenly, certain places became off limits. Many young men, who were suspected of showing attachment to the Soviet Union, disappeared. How and where they died was a mystery. We later found out that there was a large spy network that knew all about each and every one of us.

Even as a young 15-year-old girl, I was told by one officer, after the war, that he read my diary in which I wrote patriotic poems. I had read the poetry of Marianna Kolosova with total absorption and attempted to write poetry myself. To think that my efforts ended up in the hands of a spy. I can only be grateful to God that my father did not suffer for my political poems. This let him know about the standard of education and the atmosphere within our family. My father had been a White Army Officer in the Imperial Russian Army and fought against the Bolsheviks till the very last tragic end.

My father writes towards the end of his memoirs:

The 22nd of December 1922 was for us a day of deep sorrow. Not one member of the Far Eastern White Army could forget this day. It cannot be forgotten by anyone who loves his homeland, even a little. On that day the only person who did not show his tears was one who felt ashamed of his tears and who did not want to show his weakness to others. This self-possession lay with an unbearable heaviness, like a stone, on one's heart and as a result many went into shock and dazed silence....

With the arrival of the Soviet Army, life started to boil. People went from house to house anxious for the latest news. We heard that the Soviet Army had taken over Manchuria. It was difficult to comprehend that we were free of the Japanese.

In my mind, these were Russian troops - not Soviet troops. As a young person who had not witnessed the criminal acts or the terror perpetrated onto her own people by the Soviet regime, the soldiers sparked within me a feeling of patriotism and love of all things Russian, the people, the culture, the country.

Our first emotion on seeing the Russian soldiers had

been one of unparalleled joy. At that time it did not occur to me that this was the Soviet Red Army against whom my father and the entire White movement fought. But we soon realised that the army was Soviet, not Russian. We met the Soviet Army as Russians, in any case I am talking about my own personal feelings.

I heard and read that in Harbin the soldiers were met with flowers on the main square. The whole city was full of enthusiasm. We got rid of the Japanese curse, the fear of arrest and gendarmes disappeared but this was replaced by a new tragedy which took over the Russian populace.

SMECH (Soviet Secret Police) arrived and took away young and not so young. Arrests began. People were taken away without warning and no one returned. I was told that our operetta star, V. Turchaninov, after his performance was invited to a banquet and a car was sent for him. He was taken away in his dinner suit.

Priests, the teachers of the Lyceum of St. Nicholas, were arrested and taken in their underclothes. We did not know about the directive of Ezov, which instructed that as Harbinians we were all to be considered traitors to our country and Japanese spies.

Poor young women were left alone pregnant or with young children. Many waited for years and some ended up organising their life as they could. Some women, having gone to Russia met their husbands already sick, having survived their prison sentences, all under the same code.

On the 4th of September 1945 Bishop Nestor, the ruling hierarch of Harbin and Manchuria and Patriarchal Exarch of South-East Asia greeted the Russian soldiers, as liberators. Film of this event has survived. Occasionally it is shown on Russian television. He was arrested in 1948.

Word spread about rapes, theft and arrests. Families were terrified. Our family had three women, if I could be classed as a woman at that time. During the most frightening raids, Uncle Dora hid us in the barn and taught us self-defense. I was small for my age, with a childish face, even though I was already 15 years old. This did not particularly bother me - except when we, as students, needed to go somewhere in formation. I was required to march with children much younger than I.

At school I was nicknamed 'Pupps' or 'Pupsik'. This began in the 6th or 7th classes and continued throughout my school life. I was not too thrilled by this because, at that age, one wished to be thought of as grown up. However, my relatives made me look even younger in order not to attract the attention of the soldiers. I wore plaits, short skirts and looked like a 12-year-old girl.

Those suspected of collaborating with the Japanese, or those calling themselves fascists, began to disappear. Most tragically, many innocent men were victims of this repression and as a result families were destroyed. Young women were left without husbands and children without fathers.

It wasn't until after many years, during the time of Khruchev and when the road was open to the virgin lands of the Soviet Union, did some women reunite with their husbands – men who were now ill, prematurely aged and had no teeth due to lack of food and scurvy. In some cases, families were united, but in others, wives found that their men had remarried after their release and had another family in the Soviet Union. Many people disappeared without trace.

One night there was a loud knock at the door – a storm erupted over our house. In came three soldiers with a torch. Next to Aunt Liza, on the floor, I burrowed into the eiderdown, shivering as with fever. I then saw the torch pointing at us and heard the words, 'Old woman with a young boy, let's go!'

Aunt Liza was not an old woman and I was not a young boy, but the Lord saved us. However, whilst leaving, the soldiers lit up some other areas of the house and saw three women, a lady and her two nieces, and ordered them to follow them on the pretext of having to check their documents in the commandant's office.

Early the next morning, they returned – downtrodden, humiliated, traumatised and shamed. Did they manage to heal from this traumatic experience? I do not know. Our paths never crossed again.

I also witnessed an arrest. As was the practice, people gathered to 'meet the cows and their cowherds'. Once the cows had been milked and the milk put through the separator, people congregated in the square where, in better times, someone played the accordion and there was dancing. At other times, this was a chance to catch up on the news.

One such evening, a truck pulled up. Out came a local who pointed at another person, an acquaintance of ours. Our friend was immediately put in the truck. His wife never saw him again. There were countless such arrests in Hailar and Harbin.

Immediately after the capitulation of the Japanese, I went back to Hailar on the first available train in order to find my parents. A horrifying site of destruction greeted me. There were roads uprooted as a result of bombings, burnt out buildings, blackened pipes and debris everywhere. The retreating Japanese burnt their own houses, which explained why the town was surrounded by fires.

Hailar was a picture of tragedy and desolation. I saw that the station had been hit, although the platform and some small buildings did survive and they became the administrative centres of the railway. Leaving the ruins of the station I ran home not knowing what was waiting for me there.

Our little house, our whole street and all the attached buildings were in tact. The island remained untouched. Only the central part of the town had been bombed. Mama and Papa were alive, healthy and unharmed. The joy of our reunion knew no bounds.

Naturally, there was no school. The building was destroyed, the teachers were scattered. Although only four months were left to graduation, there was no possibility of resuming school life.

The war ended, fires were extinguished and unexploded bombs diffused. My girlfriends needed to look for work. Many had lost everything, houses, property, but thank God, my closest friends did not lose members of their families. All were alive, but they were left with nothing. The girls needed to work. Where would they find a job?

The town was destroyed. Offices and businesses did not exist. The only work that was available was work on the railways. So, my classmates were employed as telephone operators. They were housed in quickly restored buildings, heated by *burjuiki* (small stoves) billowing smoke, surrounded by soldiers, whose use of the 'Russian language' proved an education to the young girls who had never previously been exposed to swearing.

Our family was lucky in that our house survived. Although totally burgled, we did at least have a roof over our heads. I also wanted to work. Here, my typing course came in handy. I went straight to headquarters and put in my application for work as a typist.

I was 15 years old; short with large naive eyes and looked younger than my years. I really wanted to look older, to be an adult. They asked me how many words I typed a minute. I answered this question honestly, saying that I learnt to touch type but did not have any practice. My typewriter had been stolen six months prior.

At the desk sat a middle-aged sergeant who was typing very quickly using two fingers. He sat me down and asked me to type something. Why I was offered a job remains a mystery to me as I had no skills and little speed. I believe that they just felt sorry for me.

So, I found myself at Railway Headquarters. Besides the sergeant, all the others working there were officers. The head of the Chinese Eastern Railway was Colonel Guliaev. I shared a clean, bright room with the sergeant.

Then, for some unknown reason, I was given my own office and the title of Secretary to the Manager of the Railway. Included in my duties was the allocation and distribution of orders and the train schedule. However, because trains ran so infrequently due to lack of resources and sometimes because of a total lack of fuel, there were few orders and schedules to distribute.

I often had nothing to do. Days were spent talking. As this section consisted of officers of high rank, I never heard any swearing and never witnessed inappropriate behaviour. One day, I accidentally walked into a room where there were several people who were talking loudly about something. Upon my entrance, they immediately stopped talking and looked embarrassed. I remember that the Lieutenant Colonel Dimitrievskii even blushed. It appears that in their company they did speak in their colourful 'native Russian' but refrained from doing so in my company. I think that they treated me as a 'daughter of the regiment'. My poor girlfriends, who worked as telephonists, were not so lucky and learnt this aspect of the Russian language in all its fullness.

I met interesting people, possibly the most interesting being Captain Vladimir Panchenko.

One sunny winter's morning I was sitting at my typewriter when, suddenly, in walks a young, handsome man with blonde hair and blue eyes. His eyes looked to me like two deep blue lakes. He impressed me with his looks, which were enhanced by his captain's uniform. Behind him was his batman Jenia. The Captain introduced himself as the camp's doctor and the replacement of Colonel Gulaiev, head of the branch of the KVZD (Chinese Eastern Railway). He gave me a look of surprise and asked why he had not seen me at the hospital.

At that time, all workers of the railway were required to undergo a full medical examination. This meant that girls were subjected to the embarrassment of a genealogical examination. During these more innocent times, many of us did not know the need for this type of examination, having never heard of venereal disease. My medical was scheduled for the next day.

And so, this blue-eyed blonde beauty said, 'I do not wish to expose you to such a humiliating examination and will now give you a form saying that you have undergone the medical.'

This note is still in my possession. It reads: 'Galina Volegova is for all practical purposes – healthy'.

I only understood what this meant many years later.

Although the sign on my office door said, 'Secretary to Colonel Gulaev', my duties, were non-existent. The railway was in the process of being transferred onto the Soviet system.

There was a need to standardise the gauges, to adjust

their incline to accommodate wagons and engines and to ensure the supply of coal. The supply of good quality coal from the region of Mukden, in Fushin province, was problematic, whereas local Chalainorsk coal was of very poor quality and its supply was also not organised. Trains ran very rarely, did not follow a strict timetable and due to the lack of a regular supply of coal at stations were sometimes forced to stop till the required amount of wood could be collected to proceed with the journey.

I once travelled to Harbin from Hailar. The journey took a week rather than the regular twelve hours. So, as a secretary without any specific responsibilities and duties, my office became a place where people from various departments could visit.

My most important visitor was Captain Panchenko the blue-eyed blonde doctor. We spent a long time talking about literature and also about life (something I knew little about given I was 15 years old). Although, having endured the Japanese occupation and the stress of being separated from my parents for a whole month, I had gained some experience and maturity.

Although my all-encompassing love for my parents made me suffer, as I relived the frightening days of not knowing what was happening and my fear for their safety, bad things began to be replaced with bright moments of life. There had been many of these. School, friends, boys, interests, emotions, school concerts, picnics, and dances – all had been wonderful and joyful.

The most important joy for me was the stability within my family. The love of my parents, their behaviour towards each other, the friendship between my mother and siblings and, of course, the love and respect for grandmother Varvara Mihailovna – all created a harmony of a good solid family.

I absorbed the stories told to me by my grandmother and mother about their life in Russia, in the Urals, in Miass. I listened to my father's tales and from these I formed my view of life. It is about this life that we spoke with Vladimir Panchenko.

The war, which flared up in August, stopped us from finishing high school, our tenth and final year. We were scheduled to do our final examinations in December. In three months we would have graduated. Suddenly, a brilliant idea came to me. Not wanting to put it off, I went to Colonal Gulaev, whose office was located next to mine, and explained our predicament. I said that our final academic year was practically finished and the exams should have been held in December. I asked Colonel Gulaev to organise the final year examinations for us. He listened to me carefully and said that he would discuss the matter with the Commandant of the City. I did not need to wait long.

'Collect the teaching staff and prepare for exams' was his answer.

Here, I encountered a big problem. Some of the teachers, including the Mathematics teacher E. Volgin, had left Hailar. Fr. Rostislav then took it upon himself to prepare for the examinations. We collected the remaining teachers and set a date for exams to be sat in all subjects. We used one of the school buildings, which had survived the bombs and fires.

Having ensured the successful completion of our school life, it was time for the Graduation, or 'White Ball'. The only thing white at this ball was the paper which covered the tables as everything else had been stolen. What was on the tables? I can't remember.

A dressmaker made my dress from lace material that was somehow overlooked by the looters. My escort was Sasha Isakin, who had just completed his medical degree and was sent to work in the Hailar hospital.

The night was not without its problems as news spread about the White Ball and some soldiers decided that this was a function organised by the White Russian Community and decided to come and deal with the 'White Bandits'. How they were eventually convinced that this was nothing more than a school social is beyond me, but in the end the evening was a success with no disruptions.

It was later confirmed that our class, which completed the Russian Hailar Gymnaseum, was deemed qualified to enrol in the available Harbin Tertiary institutions and Colleges, saving us from the need to repeat our final year of high school with its newly introduced Soviet curriculum.

With the arrival of the Red Army, contact between the population of Hailar and that of the soldiers became inevitable. Some were billeted in private homes and life continued in close contact with each other. Political discussions were avoided and in our family people were accepted based on their personal attributes.

I clearly remember one particular event as if it was yesterday. It concerns the family of Fr. Rostislav Gan, whom I respected and loved. At that time he and his wife had two sons, Adrian and Seraphim, but were expecting a third child. Fr. Rostislav had said that I would be the godmother of this child. Sadly he was born with a heart defect, with no hope of survival.

Fr. Rostislav baptised the infant that night, giving him the name Alexei, and in the morning took the tiny coffin to his parish church of 'The Mother of God of Kazan'. The child was quietly buried in the territory of the church and my name was entered in the church records as his godmother – a godmother who had not even seen her godson.

As I walked down the street in tears upon hearing the news, a young lieutenant approached me. His name was Vladimir. He was very handsome, behaved impeccably and was known to the whole town as someone who attended all the dances.

'Galina, why are you crying, what happened?' he asked.

I told him about my godson.

'We must thank God that he took him to Himself now.' These were the words I heard from a Soviet lieutenant, a handsome young man, a man who by his looks did not lead one to assume such a deep faith.

Another event that remained in my memory was also

connected to Fr. Rostislav. I met in his home a man who
to me seemed quite old, although he was probably not
even 40 years old. He was a colonel in the Soviet Army. He
often visited and talked with Fr. Rostislav and I remember
seeing him in church, on his knees, deep in prayer. This
was 1945 – 1946.

Another incident happened when I was still in Hake. A
colonel and his wife were billeted next door to my home.
We shared a fence with our neighbours, the Bondarevs, and
at the colonel's suggestion, installed a gate between the two
properties. The colonel advised my parents that anything
was possible as the behaviour of individual soldiers could
be unpredictable. In the event of a disturbance, my parents
were told to run next door. On this day, four officers burst
into our home; they pointed a pistol at my father's temple
and made him stand near a wall. They ordered that the
trunks be opened and their contents to be brought outside.
Somehow my mother managed to run next door. The
colonel appeared, called the patrol, and a marauders were
taken away, leaving my parents relieved but shaken, having
survived such a horrifying experience. I remember the
colonel and his wife. I learnt not to judge people by their
appearance. She was the very image of a Soviet woman,
large in build and with a red scarf on her head, an image
that filled our journals and newspapers.

Times were unstable. The city was destroyed but life
gradually resumed. With the coming of the Red Army,
factories such as my father's were transferred into Soviet

hands and became cooperatives. My father then became the Director of the Cooperative. We lived on an island near our factory but after its closure and the transfer of all factories to one enormous building outside the town, we needed to buy a big house in the town itself. Half of the house was our living quarters, and the other half was the office.

We bought the house from M. Vorontsov. It was a large timber building in the Russian style. It had an entrance hall, a living room, dining room and two bedrooms, a bathroom and kitchen. The other half of the house had three rooms that were used as office space.

People said that this house was built for the Ataman (Cossack Chief) Semenov about whom there were rumours throughout the town concerning his private life. My bedroom had a connecting door to the office where the accountant, Georgii Smirnov, worked. Papa did not spend much time in the office as he was either at the factory or in transit.

Over 50 years later I received two letters from the brother's Smirnov. One from Yuri, a co student, and the second from his older brother, Georgii, that very same accountant.

He wrote:

In the spring or at the beginning of summer 1946, your father, Ignati Kallinikovich, invited me to work at the leather factory Collective in Kudahan, some 6 - 7 kilometers from town. Your father was the director of the factory. I remember very well the red horse and cart, our transport at the time – reliable and healthy. I remember the bicycle and the hat with corks that your father liked to wear in summer. I remember the song you sang in your home, 'All around is blue and green'.

Many, many memories are connected with this period of my life. There was an outside kitchen. It was a small cosy building, also made of wood, with a Russian stove. How I loved it! I wanted to live in it and mentally decorated it, imagining myself in the role of 'hazaika' (homemaker). But this was not to be.

I remember how I received my very first pay packet. Making my way along the street, running past destroyed and burnt buildings, I was actually running because I was anxious to bring my pay packet home. I wanted Babushka Varvara (who lived in Manchuria but was visiting us at the time) to witness my contribution to the family income. I was scared that something could happen to prevent me from reaching home safely. Many things could happen during these times – a stray bullet, an exploding mine – all was possible. Why was it so important to me?

My father had bought a new house. I found out that someone was selling furniture – a couch and two armchairs. I really wanted to buy this furniture with my own money. Although not new, it was in reasonable condition. It was impossible to obtain anything better in all of Hailar, so I was very happy with this.

I later found out that due to a miscalculation by the railway accountant, I was paid for two months instead of for one month. He was punished with a period in the guardhouse as a result and I did not receive any pay in the following month. However, the furniture was in our home.

Student Life, Work & Love in Harbin

With high school behind me it was time to continue my education in Harbin. The Harbin Polytechnic Institute was not an option because of my total lack of talent in mathematics. I was only attracted to medicine.

I set my sights on the Medical Technology Institute and the question arose about where I will be living. I was hoping that Mama would rent a room for me and imagined my student life enjoying freedom and independence. My mother brought me to the home of my godmother, Maria Feodorovna Protodiakonova, her sister.

My mother said, 'If you take Galia, I will leave her in Harbin. If you do not, I will taker her back.'

For my godmother, this was an unexpected surprise, not to mention, shock. For me, it was a devastating realisation that all my hopes and plans for independence were gone. If I wanted to stay in Harbin I needed to accept my fate and live with relatives.

My new life - catching up with old friends and making acquaintances - began ...

First, I met Vera Kornilova, who had previously spent her holidays with us in Hailar. Although she was older, we had become friends and she introduced me to Volodia. whom I first met at the age of seven. I liked Volodia very much. As a young girl, I would eat porridge every morning simply because my Mama said Vovochka 'Vova' Kornilov ate his each morning.

The Kornilov's moved to Harbin. It had been ten years since I had seen Vovochka but our friendship blossomed immediately. I was welcomed as one of the family.

Vera, Vova and their mother lived in Pristan, in a large flat on the second floor. Their father had died during the war and this had left a deep imprint on young Vova. Vova and I did meet again in Cheliabinsk after 57 years.

When I arrived in Harbin, Vova and I began to go out. He was beautifully brought up by his mother and sister and it was very pleasant to go with him to the pictures, to concerts and to the theatre. Vova his good friend Volodia Zaharov and myself went everywhere as a threesome. There were often parties in their home as his mother Vera Vasilievna surrounded us all with warmth and care.

At this time, I enrolled at the Medical Institute where I was surrounded by many young people. Life was full of new acquaintances, new impressions. Lectures started. Everything was very interesting.

Doctor Uspenskii, the director of the Medical Institute who read Anatomy, was a plump, balding man with glasses balancing precariously on the end of his nose. He was demanding when it came to tests. I remember sitting his first exam in Anatomy. I was not prepared for the test because firstly there was no time to study and secondly because I did not have access to a skull and had to rely on the illustrations in the anatomy atlas. Suddenly, the boys were in possession of not only a skull but of different bones, which they lent to each other when needed.

The Institute had only one skeleton for use by the whole auditorium. Where did the boys get their bones?

Tim Anifrenko once said to me, 'Do you want a skull? Come tomorrow morning. Don't be afraid. We will go to the Chinese cemetery and I will get you a skull.'

I must say that I studied for exams with Lidia Ablamskaya and Eric Varbola in Lidia's home and it was our combined decision to get the skull. I took a tram to Tim's place and together we went to the cemetery. It was not the practice for Chinese people to cover the body with earth after burial and because of this it was possible for the boys to find skeletons.

Tim took a large stick with a metal hook and fished out the skull. I calm my conscience with the fact that this act of vandalism was undertaken in the name of knowledge. We wrapped the skull in several sheets of newspaper and

I, tightly holding it in my hands, careful that it did not fall out during the tram ride and very well aware of the unpleasant consequences that lay ahead should our deed be uncovered, transported our bounty to Lidia's place.

Lidia already had a pot of boiling water with various disinfectants on the stove. We boiled the skull thoroughly, changing the water several times. We painted it with lacquer and became independent owners of the skull. Now there was no excuse not to pass tests and exams. When I first brought the skull to my godmother's house, she was horrified and refused to have it in her home. Eventually the skull became a permanent fixture. It stood in turn on the table, the shelf and on the widow sill. When we studied anatomy for the organs, we bought meat that we dissected. We did the same with kidneys and brains.

Among our lecturers were some very interesting and talented doctors. Dr. Fainitski was lively, enthusiastic and with a love for 'the weaker sex'. He taught physiology and resembled an actor, who in the Soviet film played the academic – Pavlov. When Fainitski explained 'Pavlov's reflex' it was difficult to believe that this was not in fact the actor playing a scene from the movie. Fainitski particularly liked to discuss Freud.

'How important is it for a psychiatrist not to fall in love with a female patient, who shared her innermost secrets, her most cherished thoughts with him and who, herself, falls in love with him,' he would say.

I remember how excited Fainitski became, how his eyes

sparkled, how he quickly mounted the podium, rubbing his hands. 'The psychiatrist is faced with a dilemma ... to respond to her feelings, is unethical as he is a doctor. To reject her love can lead to new stages in her illness.'

Dr. Goldheimer was an Austrian Jew, not handsome but wonderfully charming. He had red hair and was always immaculately dressed. He changed suits each day of the week, beginning with a dark navy one. We liked him a great deal because the other lecturers, such as Professor Shamraev, wore the same jacket each day. Dr. Goldeimer lectured on the art of diagnosis. He spoke Russian with an accent and often sprinkled his lectures with very clever anecdotes and jokes. When he lectured, the auditorium was always overflowing. Everybody listened with interest. His lectures were presented with conviction; his descriptions of illnesses and their symptoms were so realistic that many students, myself included, often felt that we were suffering from the symptoms being described. When male students began to identify gynaecological problems, it testified to our mind's ability to convince itself of many things.

Dr. Yuri Kislitsin was the son of a White General. He was handsome, with dark hair and blue eyes and thick black eyelashes. He knew the strength of his attraction and could flirt. I remember his expression when he, during a lecture, having given the name in Latin said, 'How is it in Russian – *piatochnaya kost* (calcaneus)?'

Dr. Zykovski's subject was, 'Ear, nose and throat.' He was from the region of Viatski and spoke in a very specific, colloquial way. We assumed that he was always interested in or in love with someone. He delivered all his lectures looking directly at one of his students. The rest of the auditorium did not exist. Once the whole class wanted to postpone a test and decided to send this student to his home in the hope that she could persuade him to do this. She agreed. When she arrived at his Kitaiskaia Street flat with its fully equiped consulting room, Dr. Zykovski received her with surprise. He heard her request about the change of the examination date, asked her to leave and ignored the request. All of us, including the poor girl were amazed at this result and we could never understand why, if there was no particular interest on his part, did he deliver all his lectures looking only at her.

During our third year we were sent to different hospitals to do our practice rounds. We did our practice rounds in Harbin. However, when my fellow student, Edik Avetisov, and I went home to Hailar for our holidays, we had the opportunity to visit the hospitals there. As students we were able to continue with our practice rounds even during our holidays.

My parents had been friends with the Isakin family for many years. It appears that his parents wanted Sasha to marry me and my parents were not against this. However, our relationship was totally platonic. We were friends in spite of the difference in our ages.

When I would come home for the holidays, Sasha would often call me in the morning and we would walk together to the hospital. He shared with me his most interesting cases, talked about his research into using aloe vera in the form of injections for the purpose of dissolving scar tissue and other conditions.

At that time, Sasha was chief doctor in the hospital. Among his collegues were a Mongol doctor who spoke Russian very well, a physician, optometrist and surgeon. Sasha was a general physician but he also needed to operate

Work was carried out in very primitive conditions. At first,the hospital was in the building that was the former, 'Bureau of Russian Immigrants'. They hastily installed an operating theatre, doctor's consulting rooms and waiting room. Later they moved to another building owned by the railway. This time the two-storey building had room for wards as well as the previously mentioned consulting rooms, operating theatres etc.

My first day as a student practitioner in Hailar included a 'baptism of fire'. I was to observe an operation with Sasha Isakin as the surgeon. It was an amputation of the leg. The leg was removed and thrown into a bucket.

Sasha, in the most authoritative voice of the surgeon, said to me, 'Take the bucket with the leg into the backyard and bury it.'

I was surprised but assumed that this task must be performed by me, as the most junior of the staff. I took the bucket, removed my operating gown and mask and went outside to look for a suitable place to bury the leg. During my search for a spade, a staff member came up to

me and laughingly took the bucket and deposited the leg
in the incinerator. All in the operating theatre had a good
laugh at my expense but I was not laughing. I was such
a naive innocent then and it is a trait, which probably
remains with me to this day.

During our practice rounds we had a chance to meet
and observe the work of doctors who had not been our
lecturers.

A particularly outstanding and marvellous doctor was
Nikoali Pavlovich Golubev. He was a surgeon with his
own hospital consisting of a consulting room, an operating
theatre and wards. On entering the hospital one was
met by a Chinese man in western clothes called Nikolai
Nikolaevich. The fingers on his hands were deformed. The
winter frosts in Harbin were often cruel and Dr. Golubev
found this poor man with the tips of his hands frozen. He
was able to save his life. The latter asked Dr. Golubev to
be his godfather when he converted to Christianity taking
the name Nikolai.

Nikolai learnt Russian and became an Interpreter
and Personal Secretary to Dr. Golubev. He was widely
respected throughout the Russian community and was
known as Nikolai Nikolaevich. All knew that it was only
through him that they could get a consultation with the
doctor. Dr. Golubev did not spare himself and did not turn
anyone away.

After Dr. Golubev migrated to Australia, Nikolai
Nikolaevich remained in China and his fate remains a

mystery to me. The following incident shows the kind of person that was, Dr. Golubev ...

As students, with stethoscopes around out necks, we were following Dr. Golubev during his private consultation. Our role was to observe the patient and to record the presenting symptoms.

During the consultation, the doctor would explain to us the nature and details of the illness and allow us also to listen to the patient's heart and lungs.

On a particular occasion, Dr. Golubev, having examined a patient, wrote out a prescription. The patient thanked the doctor, put money on the table and left. The next patient entered.

Suddenly, Dr. Golubev stopped everything and told one of us, 'Catch up with him and return his money.'

The doctor healed the poor without charge.

Another doctor, Dr. Hudokovski, led a dissolute life but was a marvellous diagnostician. Once, being very drunk, he was called to see a sick child of a very rich family, which occupied a suite in the Modern Hotel.

Dr. Hudokovski arrived, looked at the child and said, 'You think that only Hudokovki is drunk? No, this child is also drunk.'

The parents felt very insulted and kicked him out of their suite. It turned out that the child was indeed drunk as he was being fed by a drunken wetnurse.

These are the types of stories about this doctor that circulated around Harbin. It was said that Dr. Golubev was friends with Hudokovski and often consulted him with difficult to diagnose cases.

After graduation I got a job at the Jewish Hospital, a private hospital where I worked as a Registrar.

The history of the hospital itself is very interesting. According to local lore, the hospital was established by the parents of a young pianist, Katse, who was kidnapped and then murdered by the terrifying *hynhyzi* (Chinese bandits).

After kidnapping the boy, the bandits demanded a ransom from the boy's rich parents. They cut off his ears and eventually murdered the boy. Apparently the parents funded the establishment of the Jewish hospital in memory of their son.

My job was to interview and examine each new patient, take their medical history, make my own diagnosis and suggest a treatment plan. Naturally the doctors did not take any notice of my diagnosis, nor my treatment plan. But, this was done to give me practice. It was like an exam which I needed to sit each day.

After accompanying each doctor on his rounds, I recorded any changes to treatments and procedures in the progress notes. I loved my work and felt very important as I had my own consulting room which was the Registrar's Office.

Dr. Zavadskii worked in this hospital as a doctor/ therapist. He was large in stature and kind in character.

Dr. Goldchamer, also worked in this hospital. Another outstanding surgeon was Dr. Dombskii, a complicated and difficult personality who was an excellent surgeon and an arrogant cynic. From Harbin he went to Vancouver, Canada.

In 1972 my daughter and I visited Canada and I had a chance to meet Dr. Domskii after many years. Dr. Chaplik was the head doctor of the Jewish Hospital. He lectured in skin venereal diseases and Dr. Linder, a lovely person, was the geneacologist. Unfortunately ,as students, we did not have a chance to work with them but we were present in the operating theatre as observers.

Working in the Red Cross Hospital, I came across the charming Dr. Shulteis. He was German who spoke Russian with a delightul accent. Using the fact that most Chinese patients did not understand Russian, he would tell us jokes while examining his patients. Most of these jokes were beyond me and I was only able to appreciate them when I got older. However, many of the older students genuinely laughed.

My longest hospital assignment was at the Railway Hospital. This hospital was located on an enormous site with different buildings spread across it. There was the eye clinic, the surgical area, treatment areas, the children's section and the skin, venereal and other treatment areas.

Dr. Buhalov presided over the pediatric ward. It was impossible to imagine a better pediatrician. Children could not help but love him. He was a kind, tubby man.

He was small in stature and appeared like a round ball who seemed to be very comfortable within his shape.

As a lecturer, he convinced us that children can discern the taste of food as soon as they begin to be weaned from the breast and are being introduced to ordinary food.

Poor Buhalov was especially busy with house calls during Christmas and Easter. Children, having received their Christmas treats of nuts, lollies and biscuits. At Easter tradition dictated the need to compete with each other to find whose egg is the strongest coloured egg, so once an egg was cracked it needed to be eaten. It was no surprise that many competitors got sick.

When I first arrived in Harbin and enrolled at the Medical Technicum, the city greeted me very warmly. I made many friends, mostly boys.

At school, my friends were mainly boys. I sat with them and shared my innermost secrets and problems. My friends included Edik Avetison, my friend from Hailar, Vova Kositsin, Oleg Chashin and Erik Varbola. All these boys were platonic friends. I gave and received genuine friendship from the boys, whereas I did not trust girls, having experienced their treachery more than once. This preference for male company continued into my time as a tertiary student.

The Medical Technicum was allowed to use the Harbin Politechnic Institute auditoriums after their lectures were finished. Our lectures started at 2 p.m. and students from both colleges were in constant contact. Some arrived, others left. Some studied after lectures, some sat tests. After lectures, in winter, it was already dark and we would walk home together in a big happy group. Oh how pleasant this was!

Suddenly, a mysterious figure appeared of the scene. Wherever I went there was a student with curly hair following me. He never carried books or drawings but was always with a football, skates or football boots. I noticed that he was very handsome. Many of students believed that he looked like the actor V. Dryznikov, star of the film, 'Tales of the Siberian Land.'

Oleg Chashin told me that the mysterious figure was his good friend, a fellow student of the St. Nicholas Lyceum. Oleg informed me that the mysterious man wanted to meet me. I was tentative in my response. I already had a great group of friends whom I trusted absolutely and suddenly some untidy, badly dressed student with uncombed hair wanted to meet me. *Who is he?* I remember thinking. *No, I will not ruin my reputation,* I decided. But, fate ruled otherwise ...

One day, during a break in lectures, Oleg Chasin said to me, 'Come into the hall and look in on the rehearsals.'

The rehearsal was for Revizor ('The Inspector General') by N. Gogol. The story was adapted into a musical comedy and was being staged by the wonderful academic, Mirandov.

On entering the hall I heard a marvelous baritone singing, 'I have invited you...' Oleg then told me the voice was of his best friend, Vova Suhov, the very one who followed me around like a shadow and trying so hard to meet me.

Vova was also involved in student sporting and cultural groups, played the mandolin and guitar, organised balls for the purpose of fundraising for sports uniforms etc. The Engineering Institute had given him a room, where he practically lived, going home only occasionally.

Having heard all this, I thought to myself, *I pity the woman who becomes his wife.*

Three years later, I became that wife.

'The Inspector General' was to be performed at a big student ball. At that time, there was a curfew imposed in the town so it was necessary to fill the entire night with a programme of entertainment. As I later found out, Vladimir Suhov was responsible for the programme. He concentrated on showcasing the talents of all the sudents. There were musical performances by soloists, the choir, the student orchestra and even displays of acrobatics by sports students. But the crown of the concert was, 'The Government Inspector.'

At that time, the head of the Railway was General Zuravlev. He was very impressed with 'The Inspector General' that he called Suhov to arrange a repeat performance at the Consulate. He asked for the names of the participants in order to pay each of them a fee. Vova, of course, did not waste any time. He compiled an enormous list of participants, including people who worked backstage and general Zuraviev had no alternative but to pay up. For poor students this was an enormous financial help.

Following the successful staging of the ball, Vova organised a special party as a 'thank you' to the organisers and participants in the concert. By this time, my interest in this 'manic' student, in this Vladimir Suhov, was very much awakened and I decided to stop torturing the poor man and allow myself to meet him at last.

I vividly remember that there were two cloakrooms leading from the hall. There was a great deal of traffic with some students arriving and handing in their coats and some students leaving and collecting their belongings. All who were entering the auditorium were keen to ensure that they looked presentable.

My ritual was to always check the seams of my stockings. Vova Suhov already stood in the hall with his eyes focused on me. I saw this clearly and continued to torture him. Previously, I loudly accepted Vova Kornilov's invitation to the party, knowing that Suhov could hear. On hearing that I would be at the party, Vova Suhov beamed. It appeared that there was a chance for him.

I arrived with the two Vladimirs. Suhov met us, and escorted us to our table. This was the first time that I had ever see him wearing a white shirt. He was wearing the formal student's uniform, which was very attractive. He was clean shaven and his hair was actually combed. Instead of the disheveled person with assorted sports equipment, there before me stood a gorgeous looking man.

Our inevitable meeting was interrupted by the students who chose this moment to present him with a trophy which they filled to the brim with wine. They then started to sing *Pei do dna* (drink the lot). I realised that if I wanted to meet him I could not waste any time because he was likely to get drunk. *What do I do?*

The orchestra was playing, couples were dancing and in the middle of the hall there was a column, attached to which was Vova Suhov. With his back to the column he was moving around, following my every move. I had to free myself from my dance partners and say to Vova K. that I needed to powder my nose. Very quickly, I ran out of the hall and immediately returned. Suhov asked the orchestra to play a waltz and invited me to dance.

It was here that our romance began, and, unfortunately, my friendship with Vova K. ended. He could not forgive me for a long time − this was a pity as I had very warm feelings for him and his family.

Vova Suhov was an exceptional person. He was honest, sincere, direct, loud, active, a loyal friend a superb sportsman and talented musician. He was the soul of any party. His strictness and harshness in his dealings with fellow sportsmen may not have been to everyone's taste. I later learnt that he was both loved and hated. He did not go out with girls and he was even called into the office of Colonel Sedih who asked, 'Why do you not like girls? Why do you exclude them from voluntary work?'

He answered, 'I do not trust them because we organise balls in order to raise funds to buy sports uniforms or equipment. When I put girls in charge of the buffet to sell sandwiches and piroshki, their responsibility is to sell the food and raise money. When they are asked to dance, they accept, students raid the buffet and we don't make any money. This is why I don't like girls.'

Suhov, suddenly found himself demeaned. How awful! He – Suhov – had fallen in love. This couldn't be.

He told me, 'What do you think? I saw you and suddenly fell in love? Let us write an agreement that we are not acquainted.'

'Let's', I answered.

He wrote, 'I, Vladimir Suhov, am not acquainted with Galina Volegova from this day.'

Both of us signed the document and went our separate ways.

The next day, I arrived at my lecture, late as usual, and saw Suhov again in his formal student uniform, wearing a white shirt and with his hair combed. I proudly walked past him and lifted my hand in order to knock on the door of the auditorium for permission to enter the lecture, which had already started.

Suddenly, I heard a voice – 'It is not polite to ignore acquaintances.'

'Excuse me, but I do not know you,' I answered.

This comedy continued three times. He did not want to confess that he had fallen in love and that nothing else existed for him. He stopped his involvement in all the committees, gave up sport and started to study more because our lectures started at two o'clock and finished at around six or seven.

All that time he waited for me at the institute in order to walk me home. He found that he now had time to study as he had his own room at the institute. He did not miss any one or our breaks and came down for them. More often when he walked me home, we walked together as a group from New Town to the Pier. Sometimes he took me home perched on his bike. I can say that it was not too comfortable but it was pleasant.

At the home of my godmother, Maria Fedorovna and her husband, Roman Petrovich, we had dinner and Vova stayed for a long time. My godmother would make obvious signs yawning, but he would not get the hint. Eventually, however, it really was time to say goodbye. We both waited for an opportunity for a goodnight kiss, but Roman Petrovich took it upon himself to escort Vova to the gate whilst carrying a large bunch of keys. This was an unwelcome shock to us, but the rules were set and we obeyed.

Comedy continued at the Institute. Wherever Vova and I went, students followed us. In the corridors, in the streets, everywhere, they formed groups and sang, 'Suhov's in love, Suhov's in love.' In winter, the words 'Suhov's in love' were scratched on the frozen windows of the auditorium. I could not understand anything. What was happening?

Eventually, Vova explained. Apparently, the guys were paying him back because whenever any one of them missed a rehearsal or training session, he became very angry and let them know it. 'You can only love, but you miss training!' They were only paying him back.

Vova and I met each day. I cannot remember one day spent apart, except for holidays during which I went to Hailar to my parents. We wrote letters during this time as there were no trans city telephone calls at that time. We missed each other desperately which only made our reunions so much better.

When we met, Vova was in the third year of his engineering degree and I was in first year medicine. He proposed to me. Naturally, we could not get married, as I was only 17 years old. I convinced him that we should wait until we finished our education. This meant that it would be three years before we could marry.

Although I was very close to my parents and was an obedient daughter, Vova only had his mother. He lost his father when he was 13 years old but he nevertheless had another 'family', consisting of loyal, close friends. It turned out that I needed to go through a form of inspection by his friends before I could be officially accepted as his girlfriend. Apparently, all the girls had to go through this process.

The group of friends consisted of five young men and their girlfriends. They included Nikolai Vorontsov, Valera Godoroja, Valentin Korostelev, Voctor Golobokov,

Vladimir Suhov and Pavel Natsikonian, who was always without a girlfriend. He was the exception, the 11th member of the group. They called themselves, *Kanitel* (The Procrastinators.) No one was allowed to join this group and this often created ill feelings among the other students.

Somehow the guys managed to get a room on the second floor of the institute, overlooking the double storied hall, through huge windows. The room was technically called the 'Architecture Room' but in it a table was set and when there were social evenings or balls in the hall, all the action could be viewed from the room. Dancing couples twirled to the sound of music and how happy they all seemed. Although life at that time was not easy, we were happy.

Youth – all conquering, all triumphant – youth!

Married at last

Before we could be married in church, we needed to register our marriage in the Soviet Consulate.

I remember walking to the Consulate. It was a bright sunny February winter day. The snow crunched under our feet, sun rays playfully sparkled and the bracing fresh air added to our joy. We walked past the Catherdral and into the Iverskaya Chapel where we lit a candle and said a prayer. Suddenly, I remembered a conversation that I had with Vova some three years ago. When Vova was talking me into marrying him, I, as the only child of my beloved father, said to him that I would like to keep my surname. I wanted to be known as Volegova-Suhova.

Vova did not object, 'Fine, as you wish. I don't mind.'

When I reminded him of this, there was a 'storm'. We argued all the way to the Consulate.

'Where is your word? Where is your honour? You

promised me and now, on the day before our wedding you forget your promise,' I argued. He tried to convince me that it is not realistic and not necessary for me to keep my maiden name.

At last, I grabbed the last straw saying that my diploma was in my maiden name and here the 'drama' turned into a 'comedy. 'Diploma, what diploma. You are a professor of *kislih shei!* (a type of cabbage soup)'.

Imagine in what state we arrived at the Consulate!

Angry, we sat at separate ends of the bench in the waiting room. An official of the Registry Office called out the names Suhov and Volegova to come and register their marriage.

The official looked at us carefully and said, 'Is this perhaps a divorce?'

We went into his office. It turned out that he was a sports fan and recognised Vova immediately.

'Suhov, you certainly gave Lokomotiv a good hiding, good on you guys and with such a score...' said the official.

Neither man paid any attention to me, so engrossed were they in their talk on football and sport in general.

They continued talking for a long time until the official finally asked why we were actually there. We explained that we were there to register our marriage prior to tomorrows church wedding and that we have a problem.

'We'll sort our any problems. So, you have decided to get married?' He was using the singular form of address, speaking only to Vova.

Then, as an afterthought, he turned to me and said, 'What about your surname? Do you wish to leave your maiden name, take your husband's name or choose a totally new name?'

'I would like to be known as Volegova-Suhova, taking my husband's name while keeping that of my father,' I replied.

The official started to laugh. 'Come off it, these are remnants of the past. It is not fashionable, not realistic to be known by a hyphenated name.'

Sadly, I parted with my beloved surname – Volegov.

Protodeacon Simon Korostelev oversaw the wedding rehearsal and preparations for our wedding. We did not call him Fr. Simon, but Simeon Nikitich. He was a very bright light on our horizon. He was charming; with a great tenor voice and his participation decorated each church service. He was the father of our close friend, Valentin Korostelev, and knew that Vova, like his own son, was a keen sportsman.

Simeon Nikitich said to Vova, 'Mind that you do not come late to church. The wedding is at 6 p.m. and you need to be standing on the steps of the Cathedral ready to meet your bride. Make sure that you are not involved in any sport on that day.'

Vova assured him that he was free of any sporting commitments and that if he does find that he has something on, he will definitely postpone it.

In spite of this promise made to Simeon Nikitich, Vova

umpired a football match that afternoon. In a panic, Vova's *svaha* (honorary matchmaker and important part of the wedding party), Zenia Korosteleva, wife of Valia and daughter-in-law of Simeon Nikitich, dressed him, put him in a taxi and brought him to the church at exactly 6 p.m. Without her help, he would have been late.

It was customary to get married in the evening and our wedding was scheduled for 6 p.m.

In the morning I had to visit the beauty salon to get my hair and makeup done.

By late afternoon I was feeling glamorous and ready to go, however, I could not see clearly because of the blinding sunlight reflecting off the sparkling snow and also because my cousin, a pharmacist, put drops of atropin into my eyes. She did this so that I would have beautiful eyes with enlarged pupils. Only by evening, in time for the ceremony, was I able to see people rather than silhouettes.

The ceremony was memorable - I felt like a queen. I did not miss one moment of the church service and was fully engrossed in each prayer. I wanted the wedding ceremony to continue forever.

The cathedral choir was angelic and Deacon Simeon Nikitich, artistic, handsome and with a voice that decorated not only the Harbin Cathedral but many years later, the Patriarchal Cathedral in Moscow under Patriarch Alexei I, made our ceremony truly memorable. I thanked Bishop Nikandr who after the ceremony, came out from behind the *ikonostasis* (altar screen), in full vestments, congratulated us and pronounced the prayer, 'Many Years' for us. It was so very touching.

The wedding feast was in our home. As the dining room could not accommodate more that thirty people only relatives, the wedding party and close friends were invited.

Galina and Vova's wedding

Having legalised our marriage in the Soviet Consulate and with a church wedding in the Cathedral, we still needed to register our marriage in the Chinese Department of Safety.

Several weeks after our wedding we remembered and went into the office where we were met by a young worker who said in broken Russian that, 'The boss is at lunch. You (addressing Volodia) don't give *pilulia* (hit) madam. You can not, another madam to go to do what you know you know yourself – cannot do – I you congratulate.'

So, after this lecture, we, barely controlling our laughter, flew out of the office with full knowledge that we have done all that was necessary and were well and truly married.

Married life began. Vova already worked as Chief Engineer of the sugar factories. His office was ten minutes away from our flat and this gave the opportunity for Vova to come home for lunch. The Chinese needed the Russian engineers so much that they turned a blind eye on the fact that instead of the usual one hour for lunch they took two and sometimes more. However , the boys never remained in debt and honestly worked late into the night on all projects which were completed by the required time.

I loved that Vova's collegues came to our house for lunch instead of going to a restaurant, which was the common thing to do. Young engineers, many of whom were not married, did not have family commitments. They received fairly good wages and earned very good money when they did overtime, and left the greater part of their salaries in restaurants. I preferred to entertain them at home. It was very pleasant. The table was set in a moment as the boys knew exactly where the salted cucumbers, eggplant etc. were kept. They took them out themselves. I served, whatever God sent. The boys contributed what they bought from various delicatessens and shops. Everything was heavenly. All felt at home, no, much better than in their own homes because not all had the kind of freedom that Vova and I provided.

Volodia was very hospitable. He could not live without people and I fully shared his love of people. We had many friends, many more acquaintances. He maintained our friendships right up to the time of his death.

Over the past 50 years I have continued to correspond with and even visit old friends in Russia, Canada, America, Japan, Georgia. In 2003 I caught up with Volodia Kornilov in Cheliabinsk.

More that 50 years have passed from the time that we parted in Harbin but warm meetings, correspondence, telephone conversations continue to feed beautiful memories.

Our family life bubbled. I worked at the Jewish hospital. while Vova worked at the Sugar Factory. Occasionally engineers were required to be at various building sites. They designed factories for the extraction of sugar from beetroot. On Sundays we, the young wives, used to visit them in Chengauz, approximately one hour from Harbin. We had a lovely time there, organised picnics and in the evening, returned as a group to Harbin on the train.

The first ten months of our married life flew past and time came for me to be a mother. I found the pregnancy fairly easy. Life continued in its usual hectic manner. We went everywhere, partied, enjoyed ourselves but just in case the birth was premature, I had two suitcases packed - one was for the child, the other for me. A jeep was booked and ready from Vova's work. As we did not have a telephone at home our neighbour was responsible for making any phone calls that were needed. Everything was quite primitive compared to today.

I'll admit I am stubborn, determined, very organised and love order and cleanliness. I decided to paint the floors of our flat to prepare for the birth of our child. I negotiated with a Chinese painter, but for some reason he stood me up.

Time was running out and there was no one to do the work. I was given the address of another Chinese man. As I was the only one who knew how to find him, I decided to go to see him and offer him the job in the morning.

I woke up and, *Oh horror!* I felt my first contraction. It was six o'clock in the morning and raining heavily. *What do I do?* I thought. *Vova will not be able find this Chinese man and the floors will remain unpainted. We can't paint floors once the baby is home as paint has a strong smell and is unhealthy for the child.*

I rose quietly, not wanting to wake Vova. I put on rubber boots and raincoat, took an umbrella and started walking through dirty, slippery streets in an attempt to find that Chinese man. From time to time I stopped while I had a contraction but my stubbornness won over my mind.

I found the man and negotiated with him to do the job. I then made my way back home in the pouring rain

Vova woke up. I did not tell him about my trip to the painter but warned him that the jeep should be made available. I had a shower, got dressed, put curlers in my hair and only then ran to the neighbour, Pelagea Feodorovna, to let Vova know that I need to be taken to hospital.

Pelageia Feodorovna ran to the office. Vova was brought home by the chauffeur and I was bundled with my suitcases into the jeep and taken to hospital. Dr. Semintovski, who read lectures on gynecology and midwifery looked me over and, with some cynicism, said to the midwife to do the necessary procedures. He pronounced loudly and authoritatively that I will not give birth before evening. He said that if I could curl my hair between contractions and to make myself presentable, an earlier delivery was highly unlikely. I felt that he is very much mistaken. I had just finished medical school. We only recently learned the new birthing method based on the total cooperation of the birth mother with the doctor and I felt that I need to be taken to the birthing room, and not to be kept in a ward.

No one took any notice of me, except one midwife who was not even on duty on that day but came to the hospital for her pay. She was the mother of my close friend, Olga Godoroja. So, this lovely woman was sat with me, stroking my hand, trying to distract me with general conversation from the sufferings of childbirth. She saw that my time had come and supported me when I loudly stated, 'If you want me to give birth in the ward   I will give birth.'

Immediately I was put on a trolley and taken to the birthing suite, and so my sweet daughter came into the light of God's world.

The 1st of August 1952 was a golden autumn day. I stood near a window of my private room holding my yawning daughter in my arms. Before us was a tree whose lilac branch seemed to greet us. Motherhood flooded over me with hurricane force. Up until then I had not experienced feelings of unbounded love for a child. Fear for its life, now and in the future, flooded over me with incredible force.

Standing by the window, feeling unfelt feelings of the love of a mother, joy and union with nature, I felt grateful that I was gifted with such a memorable day. It was only ten o'clock in the morning, thin strips of clouds were seen on the azure sky which opened into the garden where I could see a lawn, bunches of lilacs with drops on rain that fell while I was probably still in the birthing unit. The rays of the sun were timidly fighting through those clouds which were still left in the sky and together with the branches of lilacs joined to bring joy and to welcome the new life. I will never forget this moment.

Although filled with joy at the time of Marina's birth, our life in China was still unstable. We lived like on a volcano, not knowing what the next day will bring. All the levels of society felt nervous. Many were preparing to go

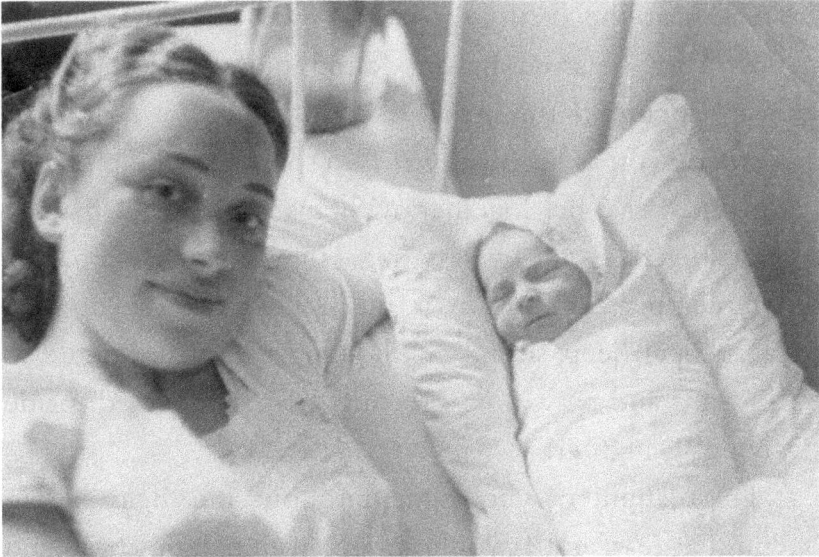

Galina and newborn Marina

to the Soviet Union, flooded with a feeling of patriotism while others were looking for a way overseas. Remaining in China was frightening.

In spite of the kindness of the Chinese to us, we could not be certain that a mass of people under the influence of propaganda against Russians would not destroy and decimate all that was dear to our heart. These thoughts and fear for the future of our newly born child scared and worried me. Although it could have been said that all the possible horrors that appeared before me were exaggerated and hypothetical, my imagined horrors did eventuate during the Cultural revolution in China.

I thank God we had left China by this time.

In writing about myself, about my happiness and my

feelings at the birth of Marina, I have not mentioned how Vova behaved having found out about the birth of a daughter. I think that like all fathers, Vova probably wanted a son as his first born. As a sportsman, he probably dreamed that he, together with his son, would play of sport together. But I was wrong. He was happy and proud. I remember how he drove me home from the hospital in an open jeep, sitting tall, holding the small bundle in his arms and answering greetings of passerby with pride saying, 'Daughter!'

This daughter, who came into our life, held me in constant fear, and I would say in an unnatural panic and fear for her life. I reached extremes in trying to protect her from possible infection and colds. I bathed her in a metal bath, which I doused with mentholated spirits, which I lit as a method of sterilisation. I boiled the water used for bathing her, cooled it to the required temperature, so that unboiled water would not accidentally get into her mouth. One could justify this behaviour because it was not recommended to drink unboiled water in China at all.

Diseases threatened us constantly. As I remember, in the kitchens of houses there was always a container with a   solution of marganese for the washing of fruit and vegetables. I breastfed Marina but when the time came to supplement her feeds, the problems increased. All the items that were used for the preparation of food for her, the plate, knife, spoon, grater, cup were initially boiled in a large pot (a sort of sterilisation), and only after this did I prepare her food. I instinctively felt that there was danger until she reached the age of one, and could not wait for her to turn one. That day came. I relaxed and became a 'normal' mother. The child grew, developed and brought joy to us.

Fr. Rostislav Gan, baptised Marina at home. Her godmother was my cousin Olga Kuznetsova and her godfather was Valera Godoroja. After the baptism – dinner at home.

Young Marina and father Vova

Everything was good, but Marina slept badly. She fell asleep with difficulty. I sat or lay next to her while she tightly held my finger. When it looked as if she had fallen asleep, I quietly took out my finger from her hand but she quickly squeezed with new strength held me even more tightly. Many advised that I should cover her and leave her in the room to cry herself to sleep.

I could never do this. I had a helper, a lovely girl called Inna, whose role was basically to give me a chance to sleep. I under-slept not only because of the child but because we led a very active life. Concerts, cinema, productions, parties, balls and sport took up much time and energy. Nothing could be missed.

The cultural life in Harbin was the key. Everything was accessible, even to poor students. We lived for the day, like most at that time. My parents sent me large parcels of food from Hailar, and we did not feel as if we lacked anything. We had a tight group of friends, five men forming the base or the group and we girls - now women - the compliment.

The first people from our group to marry were Lera Korostelev and Zenia Krypko. We were all attendants at their wedding. The second pair Vova and I. Zenia was the *svaha* (honorary matchmaker) whose duties were a combination of the best man and matron of honour to Vova. My godmother was my *svaha*. The next wedding was between Kolia Vorontsov and Rita Gritsenko and then the madly in love Lera Godoroja and Olga Bochkareva. I was Lera's *svaha* and he was the godfather of Marina. So we not only were friends, but we had became even closer and these strings of our friendship remain strong to this day.

Victor Golobkov was a very interesting and talented member of our group. We called him 'Shmagoi' in honour of the actor who stared in the film, 'Bez Vini Vinovatie' ('Guilty Without Guilt'). He was a naturally talented comic. It was enough to look at him and immediately one felt happy. He especially made us laugh when he ate *pelmeni*, taking them out of the bowl using a ladle, opening his enormous mouth and actually pouring them in like into a large cone. We doubled up with laughter. He had a beautiful girlfriend, Ira. A beautiful girl but for some reason they parted and Vitia disappeared from our group. During our trip in 1976 we spoke to him by telephone. He worked as an architect and a furniture designer. The sad news of his death came to us some years later.

The Korostelevs were the first to go to the Soviet Union. As deacon, Simeon Nikotich's life and that of his family was closely connected with Bishop Nikandr, the Bishop of Harbin and Manchuria. Our church in China went over to the Moscow Patriarchate. Bishop Nikandr directed the diocese after the tragic arrest of Bishop Nestor. The Patriarch of All Russia, Aleksei I invited Bishop Nikandr to serve in his homeland and the family Korostelev left for the Soviet Union.

The Vorontsovs went to Brazil, following the family Godoroja. Victor Golobkov fell away from our group and with him Ira who also left. They parted and separately also left for the Soviet Union. The only people left in Harbin were Vova and I as well as Pavlik Mnatsikonian.

The youth at that time were enveloped in a feeling of patriotism. We did not involve ourself in politics when there were Russian films, concerts and dances. We enjoyed music from the latest movies, danced to their melodies. Patriotic war songs reached us and touched our hearts. The

1917 revolution was far from our minds. Our native land beaconed us. Young people started to put in applications to go to the Soviet Union. There was no immediate acceptance. Some went, 'under the wire' as we often put it. Only many years later did we find out about their fate.

The Railway club house and theatre was rebuilt. Actors, musicians, singers were all actively recruited. There appeared a symphony orchestra, drama group, choir, operetta, opera and ballet company. We immersed ourselves in the best of Russian entertainment and culture.

Suddenly in front of us there was an opportunity to go to our historical homeland. Many were interested immediately. There were even such patriots who said that it is sad that they are going after the end of the war, without having been able to share the difficulties of the war and post war period with the Russian people.

My husband and I obviously wanted to go to our historical motherland. We began to dream about life in Russia (in our mind this was Russia not the Soviet Union). We told our decision to our parents.

Vova's mother, Alexandra Nikolaevna Suhova, did not want to go to the Soviet Union and behind our back was seeking ways in which to go overseas. We had no relatives or even acquaintances overseas and because of this we could not even think about it. Somehow Vova's mother acquired documents for migration to Chile. We were angry at her interference. Also we found out that the visa to Chile would only include the Suhov family and that my parents and the Protodiakonovs could not travel with us.

At a family meeting, we decided to go to Russia - even though we could not image what this would involve. My parents were told that they were coming with us. We all agreed. Suddenly, we received a letter from my father from Hailar. I open the envelope and with trepidation read the letter, which was written with a very wavering hand. My father had beautiful writing and here it was unrecognisable:

Galochka and Volodia, Tonichka and I decided not to go with you to the Soviet Union. I am an officer of the White Army. I swore allegiance to the Emperor. I cannot live in a Soviet Russia. I will never renounce my allegience. We will not stop you from going to Russia, we do not have the moral right to do so. Let this be your decision.

I flew to Vova's office. He was so enthusiastically getting ready to go to his historical homeland and my father with his decision destroyed all our plans. *How will my husband react to this?* I wondered. To leave my parents in China was frightening because there were already stirrings of things to come. We were not needed by the Chinese anymore. They were beginning to feel that they had already learnt the skills necessary to manage the work for the glory of their own country without the Russian presence. We had nowhere to go overseas.

I called Vova out of the office and he read the letter. I held my breath while he pronounced our sentence.

'We cannot leave your parents,' he said sternly.

I remain grateful to him for this decision to this very day.

By this time, Harbin was boiling. The agitators for migration to the virgin lands worked full steam. There were threats of loss of work. *How do we live? What do we do?* I questioned.

It was good that at the moment the Chinese still needed engineers. In some organisations, such as hospitals, doctors were fired. The famous surgeon, Dr. Domskii, was preparing to migrate to Canada. He lost his job in the Railway Hospital.

The agitators were very active. Some tried to ingratiate themselves with the Soviet powers, sending many families to a hellish fate whilst themselves eventually settling safely in Australia. I do not criticise people who, by their own will and by their own decision, decided to go to the Soviet Union. In fact, I respect these people. These people believed that they were driven by a higher calling to serve their own people. I feel sorry for those who did not share this patriotism but went under the influence of these heartless agitators. And there were people like that.

Harbin was divided between people who were waiting to go to the Soviet Union, those who were 'sitting on their luggage' waiting to be taken off some waiting list, any waiting list to travel overseas and some like us who were not waiting for anything as we had nothing to wait for. Then came a memorable and all deciding day in our fate ...

Vova and I went to the movies at the Soviet Club. There was a mass of people at the entrance to the theatre. All talked about their plans quite openly. Who is going where? Did they receive a visa? Were they taken off the waiting list?

Suddenly, I heard the loud voice of Nikolai Butvilo, 'Vova, what are your plans? Where are you going?'

'I don't know, I don't have anyone overseas', he answered.

Nikolai said, 'Write to Fr Andrei Katkoff, he helps many people. I will give you his address.'

This is the kind of conversation that occured in the foyer of the Commercial building, now the Soviet Club.

I must note that like Suhov, Butvillo had a wonderful voice. They could be heard everywhere and all over the place. Both were former students of the St. Nicholas lyceum and both were sportsmen.

We wrote to Fr. Andrei who had moved to Melbourne, Australia. He, like Fr. George Branchaninov, graduated from the Lyceum of St. Nicholas. There was no answer until two months later when we received a short laconic letter: 'Your documents were passed on to the correct sources, the number of your visa is such and such etc.'

In our request for migration to Australia, we added Vova's mother, who lived with us and had the same name, Suhov, my parents, Volegov and my godmother and her husband Protodiakonoff.

This news stunned us. What joy! We had the opportunity to leave China all together without leaving my parents or my godmother and her husband. All who remained in China during this period knew very well that our presence there was no longer needed.

Now came the question of obtaining permission to leave China. This was a prolonged process. The pressure to go to the Soviet Union was strong. They threatened with loss of work. 'The country has forgiven you, the borders are open,' these people said.

Thank God we did not fall for these calls, or should I say that even though Vova and I burned with a desire to go to Russia, my father, with his letter, turned our future in a different direction.

It would be untruthful to say that we made the decision to go to Australia lightly. It was a difficult decision. I was brought up as a Russian right through to my bone marrow, in a solid patriarchal family. From my youth I did not concern myself with politics, having been born in China and having grown up among Chinese and Japanese people. To suddenly hear Russian speech, Russian songs, to see Russian films was an experience which did not allow me to think of that bloody terror that the Russian people had suffered under the Communist yoke. For us young people, this country to which many people from Hailar and Harbin were going was not the Soviet Union but Russia.

But I ask forgiveness that I dared to express my feelings as being on behalf of many. It is quite possible that not everyone shared my feelings and understandings. My husband and I believed that through our choice we deprived our child of her homeland, our historical motherland. At that time, as with our parents, we had no choice. Now, after many years have passed, we see that this choice was correct.

We came to a free country where care for the individual is at a high premium. Our parents were able to live to a deep old age, cared for by both their family and the government. They lived a fulfilling dignified life and had a deserving old age surrounded by love and care.

When our daughter started school and entered Prep at Coburg Primary School, I told her, 'Marina, behave well and do not let anyone look at you as a naughty, badly behaved Russian girl.' I am totally sure that this kind of direction on my part did not allow room in the soul of my child to get an inferiority complex about her background, which often became a problem for some new Australians. Those who denied their background but, in turn, did not gain full acceptance into the general Australian culture felt inferior, but I did not have that problem.

Within our family we have two cultures, even three. Russian, Australian and Chinese and with what enthusiasm did I impart the Russian part of my culture to the Australians. But about that, later ...

We waited for our turn to be taken off the list. In Harbin no one kept silent about their plans. All shared their plans about where they are going, what they are preparing and packing. My parents sold their house. The wait was difficult. But youth conquered all.

We continued to enjoy ourselves. A very interesting thing happened in Harbin, characterising fully the kindness of some individuals and the duplicity of others. There was a ball at the Soviet Club, which was attended by many young people. At the same time there were various activities and games including a type of shooting range organised on the second floor of the Club. Upstairs there was a portrait of Mao Tse Tung. For some reason, the boys decided, obviously from youthful stupidity, to shoot at the mole of the Great Leader. No one would have known about this but next morning a teacher saw the damaged portrait of the leader, took it off the wall, wrapped it in a black material and took it to the Department of Public Safety. The boys were arrested, the parents – in a panic. Some of the families had already been taken off the waiting list and were ready to travel overseas. It was only because of the intervention of a wonderful person, who was respected by both the Chinese and the Russians due to his participation in sport and other cultural organisations, A.M. Melnikov, were the boys released and the families were able to leave Harbin. The woman who denounced the kids, and cried over the portrait of Mao Tse Tung, safely migrated to Australia, having sent many people to work the virgin lands.

The momentous day finally arrived.

Excited, Vova ran from his office to the front steps of our

flat, with sparkling eyes and flushed cheeks, he shouted, 'Galka, we have been taken off the list. Lalia Koreneva, wife of the President of the Department of Soviet Citizens, saw our name on a list on her husbands desk and immediately rang me at the office. It is still a secret so don't tell anyone.'

I hurriedly gave Vova lunch, got dressed and flew to the Kitaiskaya Street. It was a bright, sunny winter day. Happy, full of joy, wearing a mink, with the snow crackling under my boots, I rushed to the department store to purchase the already selected items for our journey. I had not been able to spend my parent's money put aside to this purpose until we were actually taken off the list. In short, the money was there 'just in case'. But, it was impossible to keep a secret in Harbin. Everybody in town knew everything about everybody, and usually any 'facts', or 'Chinese whispers' came back very much distorted. So, approximately one hour after Vova and I found out about our good fortune, I was already being congratulated by all our acquaintances - virtually everyone in the street.

Intense preparations for our journey began. Things were put in trunks. We did not hire special packers but packed everything ourselves. We did not have particularly precious things, but we did try to collect all the necessities to tide us over during our early period in Australia so that at first, not knowing what awaits us there, will there be work immediately, will there be work at all. In short, we tried to provide ourselves with clothing. We ordered from dressmakers suits, coats, bought footwear, underwear, filled doonas, dressed Marina for the first two to three years. The dressmaker, Margarita, who was very well known for her ability to sew children's clothes, was practically unreachable. She was being pulled in all directions but I was fortunate enough to secure her services for several days. She was simply an artist. She sewed girl's dresses, coats, hats, caps and she did this with such speed and enjoyment that it was a pleasure to watch how she created this tiny classics.

We continued to live our days in Harbin. The atmosphere was very nerve-wrecking. The Chinese let us know that our continued presence is not necessary for them anymore. They decided that they could cope by themselves without the Russians. If before, on all important posts, there were Russians, with the Chinese being their helpers or second in command, now they let it be known that they were in charge. When in hospitals we witnessed terrible scenes showing the work of these 'doctors' or 'felchers'. We were horrified.

For example, a young Chinese went through the same course with us. I must in fairness say that conditions for Chinese had been terrible. In order for them to enrol in HPI or the Medical Technicum, they needed to learn the Russian language because the lectures were given in Russian. This student was behind in his studies, was not very sociable and not very clean. Somehow, he reached second year and then during the period of 'enlightenment of the new China' I see him in the consulting room of the Railway Hospital with a sign on the door saying 'Doctor.'

He was the least capable student and was seeing patients in his consulting room.

Even worse, in one of the hospitals, already after the Russian doctors had been fired, a Chinese cleaner obtained a doctor's certification. Of course he had observed what happened in the hospital, saw how some procedures were done and here he was required to do an operation — to remove a tumour on the neck. He boiled the instruments, carefully laid them out on the unsanitary leather couch and began to remove the tumour. What became of the patient, neither I (nor the person who told me this story) knows. How many people died from infections and other complications is not known. But these were exceptions.

Mostly the Chinese, who received the correct education, became good doctors and surgeons. For some reason it was considered that they had small hands and with some delicate operations were particularly successful. I don't know if this is the case.

Before we left Harbin to come to Australia, some amazing things happened - one being the regeneration of icons. This sometimes happened in private homes and talk of this caused much concern in the community. But, when old icons started to miraculously renew in churches, this caused a great spiritual revival among the populace and concern among the rulers. The mass renewal of the icons on the iconostasis of the Blagoveshensky (Annunciation) Church happened in the middle of the night in the presence of one Chinese man. The old church was closed and provided accommodation for Chinese people affected by the flood. Floods usually destroyed the housing of the poor Chinese, usually leaving them with nothing. Bunk beds were set up in the central part of the old church and altar, which was behind the iconostasis (icon screen), was locked. One night, a Chinese man who had been sleeping on this bed, woke from a bright light and saw how icons, darkened with time, began to transform into light and bright colours. He woke all the other Chinese people in the church. There were many families who were refugees from the floods in the church at the time. They all became witnesses to this miraculous event. They woke the priest and this event gained a great prominence throughout the area. I heard that the witnesses accepted baptism. I was present at one of the night services and saw the icons on the iconostasis. A Commission was sent from the Soviet Union in order to investigate the phenomenon, but it did not come up with a solution. Some were suggesting that this occurred because of changes to climatic conditions. There was talk that in certain circumstances paints react to changes that occur in nature and change colour. However, no oil paintings in any of the homes showed any signs of changing their colours and regenerating at that time.

There began a constant round of farewell parties in homes and in the Club. We said goodbye to some, then to others who were departing to far away lands into the unknown. However, lightheartedness often overshadowed sadness because of youthful exuberance which surpassed all fears and concerns. We did not know English, tried to learn a little but through stupidity did not take this seriously. *What awaits us in Australia?* I wondered. *Where are we going?*

We understood very well that it was not an option to stay in China. We were no longer useful to the Chinese. They quickly stood on their own feet and wanted to build their own country. It was 1957.

Our sponsor for our journey to Australia was the 'World Council of Churches'. My parents needed to leave before us. We left several weeks after them. The sponsor reserved places for us to travel to Tiansin where we stayed in a hotel until we were able to board the ship to Hong Kong. After a few weeks in Hong Kong we would then set sail for Australia on The Taiping cruise liner.

Our day of departure arrived. Our closest friends had already left. The Korostelevs to Russia, the Vorontsovs to Brazil, Golobkov to Russia. Vova Sokolov also went to Russia. From our company, only Pavlik Mnatsikanian stayed in Harbin. Also left was Oleg Chashin, as I remember he could not decide for a very long time where fate will send him but in the end he ended up in Riga.

We went from Harbin to Tiansin. It was very touching that Vova's collegue, a Chinese and his wife saw us off at the station and gave me a Chinese purse, but before this, they invited us to their home for Chinese dumplings. This was not typical. During this time the Chinese began to avoid Russians. Even though Vova's colleague was also an engineer, he received a tiny salary in comparison with Volodia. Russian engineers received good money, whereas the Chinese in their own country needed to be content with a low wage. Memories of this Chinese family remain with me to this day.

In Tiansin we boarded the liner. Being on a ship for the first time in our lives, we dressed immaculately and went on deck. I remember how the officers of ships were in white uniforms and talked to each other in a relaxed way, were drinking coffee while at the same time ushering us onto the ship. They brought us to - *oh what a disappointment* - the bowels of the ship.

There were bunk beds with women on one side and men on the other. In fairness, I must say that the bedding, compared to the Tiansin hotel, was snow white. There was a decanter with water near each bed. Dreams of sailing in comfort did not come to fruition but this was not the worst. People could only sleep in these beds, the rest of the time had to be spent in the salons, in the dining room, on deck. There were games, we swam in the pool, organised evenings, gathered in the lounge. The bar held no interest for us as we were only given spending money for cigarettes. In truth, we did not know the types of drinks that were available in the bar. For us, the whole experience was weird and we happily participated in all activities until the first rolling of the ship.

My poor husband who so dreamed of playing deck quotes, spent three days lying down. I survived a little better but still it was not very pleasant.

At last, the ship arrived in Hong Kong - a new, unknown world. Although we had spent all our lives with Chinese people, the Chinese in Hong Kong were dressed differently. There were Chinese ladies, trim and delicate like statues, wearing their figure hugging dresses with long splits, effectively emphasising the form of the leg, with hair tightly bound into beautifully styled buns at the back of their necks. We saw a new image of the beautiful, elegant Chinese woman.

Because of the climate, or work requirements, men were also dressed differently to those in our region of China. Most men were in white shirts and shorts or in lightweight summer suits. We landed in Hong Kong in the morning and were greeted by beautiful sunny weather and a few recognisable faces, who were there to meet the ship. We were met by V. F. Riabkov, the son of my father's former Hailar factory and shop partner. My first question was, 'How are Mama and Papa? Is everything alright? Did they arrive OK?'

He answered, 'Everything is fine but Ignatii Kallinikovichwas very upset that he lost his cross in the bathroom.'

Given all our worries in making such a momentous journey, I thought that my father's concern about losing his cross, seemed a little over dramatic. Yes, the cross was gold, the chain was gold but compared with all that we have been through in the recent past this could not be such a tragedy. As I found out later, my parents exchanged crosses after their marriage as a sign of eternal fidelity and love. This is the cross that was lost.

Many years later in 2003 I also lost my cross, which was put on me during my baptism. I wore it for over 70 years, I lost it in St. Petersburg during an excursion to Petrodvorets. I felt overcome with sadness but remembered by father, remembered his loss and the sentimental feelings connected to the exchange of crosses, I calmed down and on my return home began to wear my mother's cross.

We were taken to a hotel which, by today's standards, can be considered 'one star'. The heat was unbearable, there was no air conditioner and it was impossible to get a fan.

The food was mediocre and there was no money. I cannot remember how much money we were allowed to take out of Harbin but know that it was only enough for Vova's cigarettes.

The shop windows were interesting, but we were not tempted because we lived as I now realise in one of the outer suburbs which did not provide us with any wondrous and memorable experiences. We waited for our departure to Australia.

Again, we were separated from my parents. Mama and Papa went first by airplane We sailed on the Taiping a few weeks later from the shores of Hong Kong to the shores of Australia. From Sydney we went by train to Melbourne.

Arrival in Hong Kong

Galina and parents

Vova's father,
Michael Suhov

Vova's mother,
Alexandra Suhov

Vladimir Suhov's
grandparents

Galina, aged 8

Student military training Vladimir Suhov (4th from left)

Vladimir Suhov, the sportsman (centre)

Music students at the Lyceum
Vladimir Suhov (2nd row from bottom, 3rd from left)
The future Fr. George Branch (2nd row from bottom, 5th from right,)
The future Bishop Andrew Katkof (2nd row from top, 4th from left)

Mrs. Egoroff's Music Academy, Vladimir Suhov (back row)

New Year's Eve in Harbin

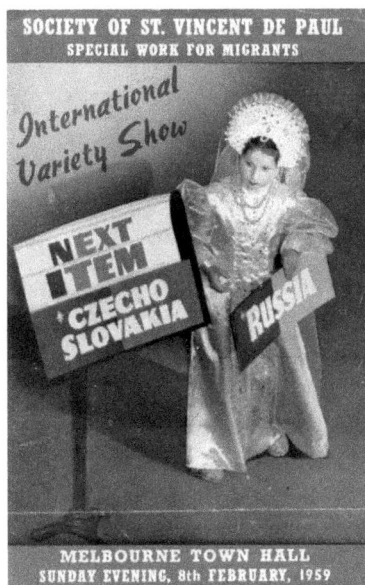

Marina in Charity Variety Show, 1959

Galina with Sr. Gerard at Sacred
Heart Hospital, Melbourne.

Russian balalaika orchestra, ABC Channel 2, Vladimir (4th from left)

Galina in Bellbrae with her father,
Ignati Volegov, mother Antonina, cousin
Vera Vinogradova and Marina

Alexandra Lupova, Maria
Protodiakonova (formerly Izergina) and
Antonina Volegova

First car. Marina with Alex Vinogradoff at the farm in Bellbrae

Fr. Andrew Katkoff and Fr. George Branch with friend, visiting the farm in Bellbrae.

Galina and Rev. Nikolay Ostianko

Marina with Vova Antonov,
Galina's cousin

Marina graduates from Sacred Heart College

Helping Marina celebrate getting her
drivers licence

Syrena Volleyball team

Galina and Vova

Nina Christesen with students of the Russian Department, University of Melbourne

Volleyball team trained by Vova

The winning cup

Basil and Marina

Ludmila Tolmacheva, Antonina Volegova, Tammy Tolmachev and Galina

Ellen and Gino's Wedding

Serge and Heather's wedding

Galina with Vera Kalman in Monte Carlo

Galina backstage with grandchildren Serge and Ellen

Alexander Shwachko, (Honorary Consul) and Galina with the Russian Ambassador Leonid Moiseev and Mrs. Galina Moiseeva in Melbourne.

Glaina and singer Alexander Malinin

Galina with Vera Kalman in Monte Carlo

Together with Ellen, visiting members of my mother's Antonov family in Miass

Cousins (Antonov family)– Evgenia, Galina and
Galina in Miass, Russia.

Galina's first cousin, Avgusta (Volegov family) with
her husband Evgeni Kolesnikov and niece Tatiana

Australia

Who or what was waiting for us in Melbourne?

The train slowly drew up at the platform at Flinders Street Station. We saw the handsome smiling face of Fr. Andrew Katkoff. The meeting was warm. Former students of the lyceum embraced each other. I met Fr. Andrew for the first time while little Marina hovered around our feet.

After the first words of greeting, Fr. Andrew took us to our temporary living quarters. This was a very simple room in a small wooden house in Coburg. In this house, my parents occupied one room; Vova's mother, Alexandra Nikolaevna, was in another and the third room was for Vova, Marina and myself. Fr. Andrew organised all this. Later, sitting on the verandah I reflected on the poverty of our surroundings. From our solidly built homes in Hailar and Harbin we found ourselves in a small, cold and sorry little house. It was Marina's birthday, the 1st of August.

Melbourne was bitterly cold. The house was not heated, our luggage was still sailing somewhere across the ocean. We did not have warm blankets, we were literally freezing. The landlady added to our difficulties. With a kind husband there was a willful, angry woman. Her husband tried to help us and give us advice. We were in a new country, did not know the rules nor the language. We needed to ask about everything, for example, the location of the bus stop, the station, how to buy a travel ticket.

I vividly remember arriving in the city and beginning to search for the Myer store. I had heard about it but did not know where it was. I stopped at a kiosk which sold newspapers and magazines. I asked for, 'Magazin Myer?' The salesman answered but I did not understand anything. He began to sort through all his magazines and tried to explain to me that there is no such magazine as 'Myer'.

'Yes, but I don't want a magazine, I want the store Myer.' (Apparently in English, the word 'magazin' means 'magazine'. Myer was a shop called the Myer Emporium.)

My mother-in-law, whilst shopping for eggs, demonstrated how a chicken went *kukareku* and formed her hands in the shape of an egg.

While shopping for food, if it was not displayed, one needed to come up with various clever tricks. For example, how to buy pepper. My godmother took a deep breath and then loudly sneezed. Or better still, my mother-in-law came to a butcher's shop in order to buy liver to make pate. She found out that *pechenka* was called liver. She walked

Rev. Katkov and Galina's mother drinking tea

into the shop and said, 'Liver me, baa … baa … ?'

He replied, 'No, moo … moo … '

So we did manage to teach some shop assistants to understand our 'language'. These types of incidents provided rich fodder for jokes and anecdotes about new arrivals to Australia.

It was difficult to start a new life. I remember how, walking along the street in the evenings I would see lights on in the houses. I was invariably attracted to the warmth within those homes, a lit fire appeared to me the height of luxury. However, in our house it was freezing. There was an angry landlady and worry about finding a job. My mother and my godmother got jobs in factories thanks to the help of kind people. How they appreciated their jobs! The factory produced women's knitwear. They rose before sunrise, travelled on public transport to the factory, with joy they received their weekly pay packets and on the way home bought produce at the market, carried it home and fed the family. My mother cooked for everyone. My godmother and her husband lived in another house not far away. So the first bread winner in our family was my mother. Then a job was found for my father at a leather factory. It made him feel good to be able to contribute to the family income. Mama and Papa were both working before our arrival.

My turn came. Fr. Andrei said to me that he was picking me up the next day and that I needed to be ready as we will be going to look for work. Even in China we heard the saying, 'on first meeting people judge you by your clothes, they judge you by your mind on parting.' Because of this, I dressed up. I put on a mink jacket and went to look for work.

Fr. Andrei brought me to a laboratory. Neither a mink coat nor high heels would have helped me had there not been an influenza epidemic at the time. Workers were hired for a period of two months for the preparation of vaccinations. The company rules were that only single women were employed but because of the epidemic, they needed to increase their staff and I got a job for two months. They sat me next to a Russian woman so as a result I did not learn one English word. We prattled in Russian, sitting on our stools and extracting from the eggs the already fertilised liquid. We sat through eight hours with difficulty, with three breaks, one for lunch and one for morning and one for afternoon tea. I must say that we arrived in Australia with an appetite fostered in the cold climate of China. There we spent a great deal of energy walking, whereas here, at a sitting job, there was not the expenditure of energy. Our appetites remained the same. As a result weight gain was a problem, although I did eventually manage to overcome this problem.

Two months went by and I again needed to look for permanent work. Fr. Andrei took me to Sacred Heart Hospital, Coburg. Anxious to create a good impression as a prospective employee, I again dressed to impress in my mink jacket and high heels. Walking into the foyer, I noticed long corridors, shiny granite floors and a statue of Christ. The hospital appeared warm and clean to sparkling. The nuns (sisters) were all wearing white habits - starched veils and long dresses. The bright corridor lead to a chapel with fresh flowers in metal, polished gold vases, an altar table, altar cross and pews for the faithful. It was different to an Orthodox church, but exuded a prayerful and holy atmosphere.

As a Catholic priest, Fr. Andrei was treated with particular respect and we were invited into a small sitting room. Immediately, a young nun appeared with a silver tea set. We enjoyed tea and delicious biscuits. (Later I asked for the recipe and make them to this day.) The sister apologised, saying the Matron was away and that we would need to return next day as she did not have the authority to hire me.

The next day, we met the Matron who, after seeing my diploma stating that I am a qualified Medical Assistant/ Midwife, offered me a job as a Nursing Aide. I needed to buy a uniform consisting of a white gown, a cap, a red cape, white shoes and white stockings. Fr. Andrei immediately took me to the city, to Russell Street, where he bought me several hospital gowns, the cap and red cape. He bought shoes and stockings. Oh, those white shoes – I will never forget them. Although they were bought in an expensive specialty store, they were heavy, hard and very uncomfortable. Maybe I did eventually manage to wear them in but during my first days on the job they were insufferable.

On day one of the job I was placed on the first floor. I could not speak English. Thirty patients were lying in 30 pristine white beds, all wearing pretty bed jackets. The maternity ward was full of flowers. Each bunch of flowers has its own card. Everything looked festive. I compared this ward to similar wards in China. The cleanliness was common to both places, but – the flowers. What else can you expect from Australia!

I was introduced to my supervisor, a young, tall and very energetic nun, Sr. Gerald. She wore a pectoral silver cross on her chest. Her cross, as well as being a testament to her belief and calling was often used to open medical packages and letters. For me, as an Orthodox, this was so hard to witness and even with no English, I tried letting her know

Galina in work uniform

that it was not right to use her cross in this way.

My shift was from 6.15 a.m. - 2.15 p.m. Together with another nurse we needed to make the beds and to hurry. All the patients had to be washed, changed and with their hair and makeup done. I did not understand the reason for the rush or why my partner would hold her hands in prayer and make a sign of the cross. Hearing the sound of the bell and seeing how staff dispersed in all directions I understood the reason for the rush. It turned out that between 7 and 7.30 am, before breakfast, the priest came to give Holy Communion to the Catholic patients. Breakfast trays were then delivered, and then the babies were brought to the mothers for their morning feeds. Vases of flowers, which had been removed from the wards for the night had to be refreshed and returned. On no account should a patient get the wrong vase of flowers. Next, I was given cleaning products and a rag and shown that I must clean the beautiful wooden doors. At first, I felt that polishing the wooden doors was beneath me as in China we had a maid to do this kind of work. However, I quickly decided that no work is beneath me and that all work ennobles the individual. There was nothing to be ashamed of and in any case none of my acquaintances will be on hand to see me polishing the doors. At the end of my first shift, I turned to the nurse with three red stripes on her cap. I pointed to the clock and gave her a sheet of paper and a pen. She understood that I wanted her to write out my duties and

Vova with friend, Aleisha Belonoshikin, in Marshall, Geelong

the time each needed to be completed. That evening, Fr. Andrei translated it into Russian.

The next day I arrived at work, not as a blind kitten which needs to be led by the hand and guided, but a person, fully confident in her responsibilities. Things became easier, although the job itself was not easy.

We were paid every fortnight. My first task was to repay Fr. Andrei for the cost of my uniform. I then bought a bucket that could squeeze a mop and a shopping trolley to save my mother from needing to carry heavy shopping bags. My mother was responsible for the housekeeping and did the shopping at the market on the way home from her job at the factory. So, having paid back Fr. Andrei and buying the bucket and the shopping trolley, I bought myself a hat. Oh joyous day!

Fr. Andrei got us a small wooden house in White Street, Coburg. It was a three-bedroom cottage with a separate dining room. However, the bath, laundry and kitchen were all in one room. There was a rather primitive boiler for the washing; a trough was used for washing clothes as well as the dishes. The toilet was outside at the very end of the yard.

What of it?

We accepted the limitations, happy with our independence and freedom from the unpleasant landlady. More joy – our trunks had finally arrived! At last we had warm clothing, blankets and doonas. I arrived home from work to find Fr.

Galina at home in Marshall, Geelong

Andrei, Mama, Papa, Alexandra Nikoaevna, Vova and Marina looking ecstatic - regardless of the fact that the entire dining room was piled high with the contents of half opened trunks. The place was a total mess but we were blissfully happy.

At this time, both my parents and I were already working. Vova, on the other hand, was taking longer to get a job. As his engineering diploma was recognised in Australia,

Fr. Andrei was hoping to find him work initially as a draftsman but to no avail. Suddenly, there was a vacancy. Keeping to the principle that, 'Clothes make the man', Vova wore a new suit, especially made for Australia, and his hat. Success! He got the job.

At the end of the day however, Vova returned home with a squashed hat and ripped trousers. His best suit – ruined. His hands – scratched. It turned out to be a laboring job on a building site. The search for work continued. Vova was employed as a leveler. Once again there was a feeling of joy at being in work. He invited one of his colleagues to dinner. Poor man. He was a young Australian man who must have been totally overwhelmed by Russian hospitality. Although he did not understand a word we were saying he knew that he was welcomed with an open heart and went away happy.

Once I understood the hospital routine and my duties, I became bored. Changing water in vases, carrying bedpans, doing the daily analysis of urine and polishing the doors was not exactly edifying work. I wanted something closer to my true profession and coveted the work of the medical sister. Finishing my own duties with incredible speed, I tried to help the sisters with their work. This included taking blood pressure, temperature of patients as well as giving medicines. Once the supervisor realised that I can be trusted with important work, in spite of my lack of English, my duties became much more interesting. There was a third year student, completing her work experience before graduating as a sister, who was not overenthusiastic in taking on her responsibilities and preferred to arrange flowers. This gave me the opportunity to take over her duties.

Naturally, things did not always go to plan and there were some amusing incidents. One time, Sr. Josephine, a lovely nun, said to me, 'Nurse Suhov, please go to Centre Supply and bring the catheter tray.' Out of the entire phrase I only understood the word, 'catheter'. She showed me the number five with her fingers and for me that meant the 5th floor. I ran to the lift and mentally keep repeating what she said. Sr. Josephine must have rung ahead as another smiling nun met me and presented me with the required sterilised tray.

Just as for Russians, Easter is inconceivable without the *kulichi,* so in Australia, the Christmas Cake is a feature of Christmas celebrations. Suddenly, I was told that I had won a Christmas Cake. Where and when I purchased the ticket, I could not remember, but I was sent to the canteen to pick up my prize. Now, I blush with embarrassment when I remember this. Waiting for me was indeed an enormous fruitcake, decorated with pansies made of icing sugar. When I picked up the cake, I was surprised at how heavy it was. I later found out that a nun who was an expert baker made it. I cannot estimate how much fruit it contained. It was incredibly beautiful. That it was a traditional Christmas Cake was obvious and it was raffled a little before Christmas. With time, this cake infuses with the aromas of fruit and brandy and by Christmas day it tastes better than ever.

Triumphantly, I carried the cake into the staff tearoom. I invited everyone working on the floor to join as I took a knife and began to cut the cake. My poor colleagues! I saw the surprised looks on their faces, their cries of protest, 'No! No! No!' but I didn't listen. I continued to cut the cake in thick slices and gave pieces to everyone. They were in shock. What for me, a Russian woman, appeared normal, for the Australians was incomprehensible. I went against tradition. The cake was meant to have pride of place on the Christmas table and to be eaten on Christmas day. Also, because it is so rich, it is cut into small pieces and not in the enormous chunks that I served. How was I to know?

We needed to learn to live in our new country. Fr. Andrei helped us a lot but it was still difficult to learn everything at once. I remember how after finishing work at 2 p.m. I went to the city. When returning home by tram I noticed a man, sitting not far away from me, slightly turn his head and give me a wink. I was furious. 'What a bastard!' He continued to wink and was now giving me a smile. I was ready to slap him but thankfully he left the tram at the next stop. On returning home, I found Fr. Andrei waiting there. I was furious. How rude for a man to behave in such a manner on the tram. Fr. Andrei laughed.

I could not understand a thing. 'What's so funny?' I asked him.

Apparently the man was just saying, 'Hello.' Winking was an old habit, which originated among Australian convicts. When these convicts, who were transported from England either deservedly or for 'crimes' such as stealing a loaf of bread, were forbidden from talking to each other, they developed the wink as a greeting among themselves.

Many years later we were in Tasmania and visited Port Arthur. There, I understood everything. Imagine if I had answered the elderly man's greeting with a slap!

In spite of my lack of English, I did not have any problems performing my duties in the hospital. My training allowed me to understand the condition and needs of each patient and even my limited experience in Harbin, gave me ample experience in clinical matters. In China, each sister gave injections, however, in 1957-58, nursing sisters in Australia were not allowed to do this. Only doctors or laboratory assistants, who came to take blood for analysis, were allowed to give them. In emergencies, when there was not doctor, there was panic. The patient's arm was already full of needle marks through the ministrations of an inexperienced sister. I wanted to offer my services and did so timidly. This was an emergency. They allowed me to try. The task posed no difficulty for me. I had the experience. From then on I was always called upon in similar situations.

Trying to get the required rest was the hardest for me. I had a 20-minute walk to work and getting up at 5 a.m. was torture. I was not used to going to bed early. Having stayed up late, I would go to bed in fear that I will not fall asleep.

Often I only managed to fall asleep close to morning and then I was sleepy walking to work. My afternoon shift was easier, 2 p.m. - 10 p.m., but my regime was still disrupted and I began to suffer from insomnia. It was horrible.

Our whole family began formal English classes but because of my changing work schedule, I needed to stop. Marina was often sick. She constantly caught colds and then whooping cough. All in all, we were not able to learn English formally. At this time, Sputnik was also sent into space and almost all Australians were aware of the existence of Russia.

Unfortunately, the factory where my mother and godmother worked burnt down and they both lost their jobs. My father, who initially worked in a leather factory, became allergic to some of the chemicals used and also needed to resign. He was very upset about this because he knew that at his age, he would not be able to find work again.

Vova and I were already working but my parents felt useless and suffered a great deal because they were unable to contribute to the family finances. Vova thought that by buying a small farm, we could give my parents an opportunity to feel needed and to be independent. Buying a farm on our minute savings was difficult but still possible.

Our good friend, Alex Alexandrov, took us to Geelong. At that time, we did not own a car. We found a small farm in Bellbrae, approximately 25 kilometres from Geelong. There was a small-unfinished house on the 25-acre site. There was one enormous water tank and two dams. The farm had four cows. We signed the documents, paid the deposit and then had to buy a car. Our first car was a Morris panel van. It was old, with paint peeling off it. I don't know how Vova managed to get a driver's licence but this he did. He drove slowly, hesitantly and constantly kept fixing his panel van.

I was happy to learn that Sacred Heart Hospital had a sister hospital in Geelong. I put in my resignation and received a reference. Since I could already speak basic English and somehow write patient progress notes and other documentation and with 18 months work experience behind me, I confidently took my reference to Holy Cross Hospital and was hired to start immediately. Unfortunately, Vova still needed to complete his contract in Melbourne so I was offered a room at the hospital. Marina lived with my parents on the farm in Bellbrae. She attended Bellbrae State School, a tiny school with only 25 pupils, breathed fresh air and ate beautiful fresh food prepared by my mother. Her health improved and she became a strong healthy child with a rosy complexion.

Young Marina on the farm

Holy Cross Hospital was tiny. It was the former home of a very rich family, the Kelly's. The Kelly sons owned a large auction business in Geelong. Our paths would cross often. At first they were needed for basic household items such as furniture. Later, when our disposable income increased, we went to Kelly's for paintings, dishes, jewellery etc. My working life at Holy Cross Hospital was much easier and simpler. I could sleep till 8 a.m. for a 9 a.m. start. Breakfast was always ready; my uniform was ironed and starched. I worked on the wards. Looking after patients was an absolute joy. There was constant contact with people, conversations and plenty of opportunities to practice speaking English. I loved it all. To my great surprise, Sr. Gerald, the nun who had been in charge of the maternity ward at Sacred Heart Hospital in Melbourne, had been transferred to Geelong. Previously, we had a rather difficult relationship. She could be irritable and harsh, and in my opinion, unfair. During our altercations, I could not explain or defend myself because of my inadequate language skills. I knew my job but my poor English obviously annoyed her terribly and she often drove me to tears. I could not understand not only her unfairness but also the fact that, as a nun, she still allowed herself to behave in this way towards me.

One day, after one of her regular blasts, she called me into one of the storerooms and closed the door behind her.

'Forgive me, I am unfair to you. I often offend you,' she said. 'This is not really how I am but it is because my nerves cannot stand it. I find it very hard to work. I have an enormous workload with responsibility for the entire floor with 33 patients. My staff is made up of new arrivals with very limited English. Please understand me and forgive me.'

Naturally, I forgave her and suddenly found myself working with her in Geelong.

Under her management, everything went very well and I continued to live close to the nuns. The hospital was old but very clean – spotless and shining. Thin walls divided the rooms. The chapel was between the dining room and the wards. There was a refectory where the sisters had their meals and spiritual discussions. I had the entire lives of the sisters - prayer, work and meals of the sisters in the palm of my hand. The nun's habit consisted of a starched cap on the head to which was attached a long veil. This was already slightly modified as their original habit included a 'bib' – also starched; a starched cap and the sides of the veil were also starched. The nun could only see what was in front of her. This may have been suitable for someone leading a contemplative life but was not practical for a nurse. She needed to use a stethoscope and to be free to listen to the baby's heartbeat during labour. Each step in changing their habit was discussed at length and required petitions to be sent to the Vatican. What happiness! They were eventually able to replace the starched veil with a soft material and their dress was shortened in order to avoid being tangled in the long skirts.

On Sr. Gerald's recommendation, I was transferred to the operating theatre. A 70-year-old German nun ran the theatre. She was short in stature but energetic, active, slim and who had never once been sick in her entire life. She had never felt the need to take a headache tablet nor medication for any other pain. She eventually became Mother Superior and her robust health meant that she could not empathise with the other sisters if they became unwell.

Operations were mainly tonsillectomies, the removal of adenoids, appendectomies, as well as gynecological operations and some others. Patients were anaesthetised using chloroform and ether. At that time ether was still dripped onto a mask in order to put someone to sleep. At first I was only trusted with the simple operations such as tonsillectomies, but I became very bored with them. I began asking Sr. Zachary to let me assist even with a simple appendectomy. At last I got my chance with Dr Grey-Thompson.

Sister said, 'Dr Grey- Thompson is a gentleman and he will be kind to you.'

I had a Russian reference book, 'The Bikov Guide to General Surgery', which explained each operation in detail. There were photographs of all the instruments and a step-by-step guide to each operation.

When my time came to assist Dr. Grey-Thompson, I was not nervous. I had all my instruments laid out and handed each instrument as needed without being asked.

Sr. Angelina

Both the doctor and Sr. Zachary were surprised and from then on I assisted in all the big, complicated operations. I made sure that I did my homework before each session.

Life rolled on and with it my English language skills began to snowball. My professional life became more varied, interesting and much easier though not materially. But, there were still difficulties. Our farm was some distance from Geelong (25 kilometers) and with only an old and unreliable car; it was impractical for us all to live there whilst working in Geelong.

Alas, we were separated as a family. Once Vova got a job in a private building company as an engineer, he and I rented a small flat near the hospital. Marina lived with my parents on the farm in Bellbrae. We travelled to the farm twice a week. My mother milked the four cows that were on the farm. She made sour cream and cottage cheese and sold these to a delicatessen in Geelong. This allowed her to contribute to the family income. In China, my mother had her own maid. To produce her dairy products, she had her own cow – but she had staff do this. Here in Australia, my father and mother needed to work together – and work hard. But they seemed happy to do this and were excited to be building a new life in a new country.

Although life on the farm ensured that our daughter grew up to be a healthy child, it was not a very happy time for me as I missed her terribly. No matter how good it was to live in an ecologically clean area, near the ocean – life away from one's child grew impossible to handle and we eventually managed to sell the farm and the whole family united in Geelong. There was little help from the government so we took on the challenge of establishing ourselves in this new multicultural country. We paid off the debt for our fare to Australia and saved for a deposit. After we sold the farm we were able to buy a small house in Geelong.

We swapped houses with a lovely Polish family. They wanted to live on a farm and were happy to move to Bellbrae. We took over their house in North Geelong. The future Pope John Paul during this time was a Polish Cardinal who came to Melbourne for the Eucharistic Conference. He was invited by this family to visit their home. So, we can boast that the future pope actually visited our farm. However, we did not meet him.

During this time we took out a second mortgage and bought an unfinished house in Marshall. Only the outside bricks, the roof and the windows were in place. The house was surrounded by nine acres of land and felt isolated although it was only 10 minutes from work. As we had little money work on the house was progressing slowly.

That year there was a terrible drought. Having spent the Christmas break with Marina and my parents, it was time to return to work. It was the last day of our holidays. I put on a swimsuit, took a beach towel, a book and some matches. I thought I would burn the rubbish whilst sunbaking and reading a book. Vova told me not to do this, as all the grass around the incinerator was dry.

"We are going back to work tomorrow and I am not prepared to cultivate flies," I answered.

Vova did not have a chance to stop me when I lit the match. Suddenly. a spark flew out and the surrounding grass burst into flame and started spreading across the field. Vova was helpless. We did not have a telephone. I started shouting, "Fire, fire!" The fire spread to the end of our paddock and up the electric pole. By this time, the fire brigade arrived, then the police. It was Sunday. It was a Day of Total Fire Ban. Starting a fire on such a day was punishable by 2 years jail, 200 pounds or both. What horror! I was an arsonist. There will need to be a trial.

Time passed. The whole hospital knew about what happened. The doctors laughingly promised to visit me in prison with flowers. A police officer came to the hospital asking for me.

"Are you Mrs. Suhov?"

"Yes, unfortunately I am," I replied.

He informed me of the court date saying that I did not

need to attend and will be informed of the outcome.

"I'm sorry," I said. "I would like to be present at court."

"Certainly, that is your right," he answered.

The day arrived. I have seen television programs where people dress especially well for court so I put on a silk dress with matching green shoes, bag and gloves. The only thing I chose not to wear was a hat. I arrived at court full of people, most of whom with driving offences.

When asked how the plead, most said, "Not guilty."

When it came my turn, I answered, "Guilty."

I could not understand everything that the policeman and fireman were saying but by the tone of their voices it felt that they portrayed me as someone who did not care about what happened. The policeman's tone was different to the one he used with me when he was trying to calm me down saying that I should not worry and that everything will be all right.

The judge asked me if I would like to say something.

"Yes," I replied. "I did not know that there were Days of Total Fire Ban. However, logic should have told me that this was not the time to light a fire. Even my husband warned me about the danger and I did not listen to him. We had just arrived at this house having been away and had no access to the radio as we were as yet without an antenna. We did not have a chance to buy a newspaper. This is all I can say."

Suddenly, the policeman and fireman who had just portrayed me as an uncaring New Australian came up to me and began to congratulate me. I could not understand why. They lead me away to pay my fine. The fine was twenty pounds, not 200 pounds. I could not understand a thing.

The clerk responsible for writing out my receipt looked me in the eye and repeated my offence as it was written on the form in front of him. I lit a fire was on a Sunday which also happened to be a Fire Danger Day. The fire spread across the entire nine acres and even touched an electric pole. Both the police and fire brigade attended the scene. It took the clerk a long time to understand why I got only a symbolic fine. After a while he came up with his "clever" explanation. "It is because you are a woman," he said. "Maybe it was because I was honest," I answered.

Life soon became normal. Our daughter went to school and Vova and I worked. My mother looked after the house. and Vova's mother, Alexandra Nikolaevna Suhova, married and stayed in Melbourne. We were in the process of bringing the rest of my mother's family from China. They included two brothers who had never married, Diodor and Nikolai, their sister, Elizabeth (Liza) and their youngest brother, my godfather, Constantine, together with his wife, Lidia (nee. Zlobina) and their son, Vladimir. Vladimir (Vova) later became an architect, married Penny, a lawyer who had studied Russian at Melbourne University and had three children Svetlana, Edward and John. Music has played a great part in that family's life. The Melbourne based balalaika orchestra; 'Sadko' had several members of their family among its ranks.

Geelong's Russian community included mainly people who migrated from Germany after the war. They were contracted to work on selected government projects and although many of them had been professionals, such as doctors, they now had to work as laborers in this new country. We would often hear snide remarks that our introduction to Australia was much easier as we were not constrained by contracts. However, we were obliged to repay the Union of Churches for our passage and we worked diligently to honour that debt. With time, our child grew and we gained experience and confidence to take up our place in this new land, our new home.

Life continued on and it was time for us to become Australian citizens. The ceremony was conducted by the then Minister of Immigration, Mr Hubert Opperman. The was the same Sir H. Opperman, also referred to as 'Oppy', who was an Australian cyclist and politician and who was internationally famous for his endurance cycling feats. In his speech he said, 'I wish to congratulate you on becoming Australian citizens. I hope that you will grow to love Australia but ask that you do not forget your own traditions. Develop them and introduce them to the rest of the people. That way, you can enrich our country. Our land is young, but we already have traditions and a history. Do not discount them. Remember that the more ingredients that there are in a Christmas fruitcake, the tastier it is. Our multinational country is enriched by immigration, by your traditions.'

His words resonated in my heart. To this day, I continue to introduce my friends to Russian traditions. Many friends have enjoyed being invited for a Russian meal, tasting our traditional dishes, learning to drink vodka from shot glasses whilst not forgetting to propose a toast, listening to Russian music, dancing and singing Russian songs. Guests learnt something new and had a lot of fun in the process. Marina spoke Russian at home and was immersed in the culture of the 'home country'. I believe that she never felt intimidated by her background. However, our lack of knowledge about how to facilitate social contacts that would enhance school life and friendships, and my inability to participate in activities such as 'tuck shop duty', meant that my daughter did miss out on many things commonly enjoyed by children growing up in Australia.

Work at Holy Cross Hospital continued. While the new hospital was being built, we worked in the old one. It was small and looked like a field hospital. At last, the new hospital was finished. We completed our operating list in the old 30-bed hospital on Friday and on Monday began work in the new. All three operating theatres were equipped with the latest technology. What bliss! There were big windows stretching the entire wall of the hospital as research showed that people who worked in an environment with only artificial light were prone to depression. Many years later, when forced to work in an operating theatre without access to natural light, I appreciated the foresight of our Geelong architects.

The old Holy Cross Hospital

Work in the new hospital became even more interesting and diverse. I loved my work. New staff, secular staff, began to populate our surgical community. Whereas previously I only worked with nuns who never swore, my education began in earnest. Suddenly, I began to hear totally new words. With an innocent expression on my face I would ask the meaning of some word or would use a word quite innocently and find that it had a double meaning. My conversations and expressions provided much merriment for the doctors and staff and I developed quite a reputation throughout the town without even realising it. Galina became famous not only in Holy Cross Hospital but also in the operating theatres of Geelong Hospital and other places. I featured in many jokes. Jealous wives of some doctors thought that I made mistakes on purpose in order to get attention. How could they understand that working with nuns had shielded me from the general environment and that I genuinely was 'an innocent abroad when it came to the secular world? Thank God I did not get offended when I became the source of laughter. The mood lifted with the laughter and I was happy.

I grew to know the habits of individual surgeons, their personalities and their techniques. So I was prepared for each operation. Kevin Coleman operated on Mondays. His list was usually very long, six to seven operations from 8 a.m. to about 4 p.m. Many nursing sisters and young surgeons were in awe of him and found his difficult and demanding nature very challenging. He did have perfect manners, had the reputation as a staunch and respected Catholic and was an established member of Geelong society. He made staff nervous and many lost confidence and were often unable to perform at their optimum level, which only exacerbated some situations. I became his constant assistant. He did not intimidate me and we developed a very close and respectful working relationship.

By nature he was an actor. He could be performing one of the most difficult operations but make it appear easy, quick and simple. There was not the drama that we were used to seeing in American films where at the first request from the surgeon for a scalpel the nurse already needs to wipe the perspiration off his brow. I was not one, but three steps ahead of him, I knew him so well.

The anesthetists were also marvelous people. Dr. Darby was a gentleman – quiet, dignified, still very handsome with luxuriant, grey, wavy hair. He spoke slowly. Often I would ask him a question, continue working and even become immersed in another totally different conversation when I begin to hear his carefully measured answer.

Another anesthetist, Richard Hallows, was a young man, not particularly handsome but with vibrant eyes. He was not only inquisitive but also curious. He was known to lengthen the rubber hose that carried the gas from the machine in order to look out of the operating theatre and to see what was happening outside. I remember Richard fondly. He died, still young at 50, whilst on morning run along the beach.

Dr. Bill Crosby – what an exceptional individual. He was a marvelous anesthetist, the Director of Anesthesiology throughout Australia and the Asian Pacific. He was demanding, strict but fair. People feared and respected him. I had a rather interesting relationship with him. He knew my religious affiliation to the Russian Orthodox Church and my negative attitude to Communism. He always began discussions with me arguing from the point of view of an atheist about religion and from the point of view of a communist, when talking politics. Our conversations were often heated and he even gave me a copy of Mao Tse tung's, 'Little Red Book'. Even to this day, I am not sure whether or not there was an element of teasing in his 'arguments' with me. But one day, he said to me, quite seriously, 'Gali, if you believe in God, I envy you. I would like to have faith, but cannot.'

Poor thing. He died of leukemia without having reached old age.

Many interesting characters left a deep impression on my life. Bob Waterhouse, thin, severe, strict, putting fear into the timid. He was a wonderful surgeon and my inspiration in the field of art. Once, during a long operation in which I was not actively participating but was only present, I noticed how Bob, having finished an operation in the next-door theatre, was taking off his gloves. His whole figure tempted one to try to capture him on paper. Tall, stooped with raised shoulders, wearing a mask and a white hat. Without realising, I captured his likeness with several strokes of the pen. I showed my sketch to one of the doctors who exclaimed, 'Bill! Show him! He will be pleased.'

I could not believe my ears. He actually recognised Bill. *Can I really draw?*

I rushed home, anxious for the evening news. Our Premier at that time was Henry Bolte. He was endearingly ugly.

He looked like a koala and was a favorite of cartoonists. I sat in front of the television with paper and pencil at the ready. Suddenly, the Premier was before me. I hurried to capture his most important features and to my great joy – success! Having never drawn before (besides a childhood depiction of a house, next to which a cat sitting with his back towards the viewer, because it was easier to draw a cat that way and a dog – two circles – four legs, smoke coming out of the chimney, a winding path and some flowers) I now found that I had the ability to draw. I began to take lessons.

Work continued to be marvelously fulfilling. There was harmony and stimulation and sometimes I felt that they should not be paying me but that I should be paying them.

We often had workmates to our home. Sometimes we invited only the nuns. They really enjoyed themselves within our family. Many photos remain of those fun times. Sometimes we invited other, secular staff often mixing the doctors and nurses. I did this on purpose as Australia was not unknown for its snobbery during those times.

The type of relationship that I enjoyed with the doctors was something that Australian nurses could only dream about so I attempted to destroy the invisible barrier that existed between them. Obviously hospital management noticed this and invited me to organise a dinner dance for all the workers of the hospital. For me, this was not a difficult task at all. I chose a very beautiful mansion normally used as a wedding reception venue. I chose the

Sister Cornelia, Galina and Monsignior Murray at the
Holy Cross Annual Dinner Dance

menu, the music and began to invite the guests. Doctors
with their wives, staff members of the entire hospital, from
nuns, sisters and nurses, kitchen staff, office and people
from all the departments in the hospital were welcome.
Everyone had the opportunity to mix and the previously
unattainable surgeons became less untouchable. Tickets
were easy to sell. All had such a good time that the dance
became an annual tradition with guess who as the organiser.

Although each year I was formally and often apologetically
asked to undertake such an 'onerous' task by the Director,
I wholeheartedly agreed as for me it was a most enjoyable
and effortless task. All were glad to get out of their uniforms,
shed the operating theatre 'glamour', dress up and party.

I was always looking for ways to 'advertise' all positive

things that were Russian. For the doctors, this opened up a new world – a new understanding of what it is to be a Russian person. Previously, all they knew about Russia was the press version of the Soviet Union. Some Australians had read Tolstoy, some knew about Pushkin if only through the opera, 'Eugene Onegin' and, of course, many people knew Tchaikovsky whose music was international. Suddenly, they were confronted with Gali. The hospital employed several Russian women as a result of my recommendations and they became valued members of staff.

One of my colleagues, also a theatre sister, was Muriel Ermert. She was married to Conrad, a colonel in the Australian Army. One day we are invited to dinner at their home in the Queenscliff Army Barracks. Muriel was very direct saying that she wanted to introduce me us to her husband, Conrad, and to a brigadier. The Queenscliff Barracks was originally built in the nineteenth century as a defense against possible Russian attack ,which never eventuated. Officers and their families lived there for approximately two-year periods before again being transferred to Canberra, Singapore, England or other bases. The brigadier was apparently interested in Russian history and culture so Muriel decided to give him the pleasure of meeting some real Russians. Although his English was more than adequate for work and sport, Vova did not enjoy the small talk that is usual around a dinner table, so he was a little nervous about accepting this invitation. We arrived and it was apparent that Vova and Conrad immediately liked each other. Then Vova saw a mandolin and picked it up. Conrad reached for his guitar and they began to play. This was the beginning of a very strong friendship, which has lasted to this day. The brigadier and his wife enjoyed themselves were soon invited to our own home for dinner. The evening was a success. Much Russian food was eaten and even more vodka was drunk. The evening culminated with the men insisting on lighting a samovar the old fashioned way, outside, with wood chips. We had plenty of hot water for tea.

Working hours were long, over 40 hours a week. We also needed to be on call for emergency operations. Often I did not get enough sleep. One of my co-workers, Trixie, a wonderful young nurse, once fainted from exhaustion. She was admitted into hospital and spent a couple of days sleeping. I never fainted, thank God, but sometimes there were some interesting situations.

One night, I was woken by the telephone. There was an emergency caesarean section. I jumped out of bed, called a taxi and rushed to hospital. The operating staff included the surgeon, the assistant doctor (who followed the progress of the pregnancy), a theatre sister, (in this case me), a sister scout to fix the light and do all the non-sterile work, the anesthetist and the pediatrician to receive and check the baby. This night, our assistant doctor, Rina Batt, fainted. All were busy with the operation. All were concentrating on the immediate needs of the mother and her baby. Poor Rina was left lying on the floor with staff stepping over her. Only after we delivered the baby and heard its first cry, were the anesthetist and scout nurse able to tend to poor Rina.

In spite of the difficulties, the atmosphere at work was good. In 27 years we did not have one fatality. There were no dramatic instances such as instruments being left in the patient resulting in big court cases as happened elsewhere if newspaper reports are to be believed.

My work schedule precluded me from reading the newspapers. Television news was not enough to satisfy my curiosity. I found a wonderful way to expand my knowledge. When the main part of any operation was over, after the needles, gauze and instruments had been counted (there were three such countings with everything noted and signed off by the scout nurse), I would calmly start some sort of discussion about either politics or religion by posing an innocent question to Kevin (Coleman), 'What is your opinion of such and such...?' He would think hard and slowly begin to answer. The assistant surgeon would also offer his opinion, as would the anesthetist. It became a round table discussion around the sleeping patient.

The surgeon who worked on Tuesdays, Frank Connolly, loved to argue and I liked to argue with him. Tuesday postoperative discussions began to be known as 'Galina's Conference' after a TV program of a similar name.

Thursday – gynecology. Sandy Kelso was tall, well built with an elaborate hairstyle. He had a tendency to be snobbish and expressed his opinions in a colorful way. He always insisted that I assist him and should he be placed in a different operating theatre, behaved abdominally towards the other nurses. The instruments would be wrong, the stitches not right, and the light was pointing in the wrong direction. I remember how Sr. Rosaria ran up to me saying, 'Gali, quickly go and calm Kelso down. He is driving everybody up the wall. Cheer him up.' I was able to do this quite easily. Even behind the mask, you can see that he is smiling and everything is back to normal.

Many years later, after my husband Vova's unexpected death in 1981, Sandy was the first man to propose marriage to me but at that time I was not ready to take such a big step.

Kevin Coleman also could not stand anyone else assisting him so when I went on holidays he did not spare the other sisters with his demands and capriciousness. According to them, only Gali knew what he demanded. Kevin also died.

After I moved to Melbourne following Vova's death, some 15 years after I left Holy Cross Hospital, Kevin came from Geelong with his wife Rosemary, a well-known artist, in order to meet my then new husband Vadim and to see me. It was a very touching meeting but not the last one. Vadim and I visited him in Geelong. His time was near and another life ebbed away. But as often happens, some people leave and others take their place. Kevin often invited a young doctor who was doing his internship to assist him. Wayne Morrison was a well-mannered, quiet and gentle person. He assisted Kevin in Geelong before moving to Melbourne.

After a period of time, Wayne began to return to Geelong as a plastic surgeon. As a specialist he remained the same humble, accessible and brilliant surgeon. I was fortunate enough to assist him with very difficult operations on two separate occasions. Occasionally, I have seen this silver-haired yet young professor on television or in the pages of medical journals and have always felt very pleased to follow his career.

It does feel very sad to receive news about the death of some wonderful very young people.

Geoff Royal was a young, talented surgeon. He was not a professional actor but on completing an operation would often begin to rehearse his role in the pantomime staged annually by Geelong Hospital. He was ambidextrous and could perform all the necessary tasks during an operation using either hand. He could even write with both hands simultaneously moving from the last letter to the first. Leonardo da Vinci could write like that. And yet sadly this young, talented man, a father of a young family, died of a brain tumour.

Christmas was a particularly special time at Holy Cross Hospital. Several days before Christmas, presents began to arrive from the doctors. Usually they included champagne, chocolates and biscuits. On Christmas Eve, after finishing our operations in all three operating theatres and with the last patient safely sent back to the wards, all the operating staff gathered in the recovery room with the doctors. Champagne was uncorked, glasses were filled and everyone celebrated. We all brought a plate of food for the party and my contribution was usually *pelmeni*. I brought them already boiled and fried them up on an electric hot plate. The Australians loved them. During these occasions the role of hostess often fell to me. I still fondly remember these happy moments, which alas cannot be repeated.

Life in Geelong

When Marina finished primary school, we were faced with the serious question of finding a secondary school for her. There were three possible private schools in Geelong, an Anglican, a Protestant and a Catholic school. There was a government school but there was a commonly held belief, possibly justified that it lacked discipline, the classes were overcrowded with 50 students to one teacher. In the fee paying private schools the ratio of students to teachers was much lower and students could have more individual attention.

After long discussions, my husband and I decided to send Marina to Sacred Heart College, Newtown, a Catholic girls school. Since my husband graduated from the Catholic Lyceum of St. Nicholas in Harbin, together with many other students, none of whom were coerced to leave Orthodoxy and become Catholic, we decided on this choice. In fact, out of all the students who went to this school, only two became Catholic – Fr. Andrew Katkoff and Fr. George Branch (Branchaninov).

Bishop Andrew Katkoff

Historically, Orthodox and Catholic clergy were wary of each other and because of this some of our Orthodox clergy decided to warn us to 'be careful of the Catholics'. We were only able to come to Australia because of Fr. Andrei Katkov. He brought out our whole family. Besides Vova, myself and Marina, there were my parents, my mother-in-law and my godmother with her husband. Potentially, we brought with us five pensioners. For this we will eternally be grateful to Fr. Andrei. And here, some Orthodox clergy started to worry about our relationship with the Catholic faith.

The future Head of The Russian Orthodox Church Abroad, but then Archimandrite, later Metropolitan Filaret, on a visit to Australia served Vespers in our Geelong parish. He gave a sermon which was clearly directed at our family as we were closely associated with Fr. Andrei and Fr. George, Vova's friends and former students of the Lyceum. Fr. Filaret was very adamant in explaining that whilst their Eastern Rite services may appear to be Orthodox, that they are in fact Catholic and that we must be very careful not to be misled. He used the example of a false coin saying that in China we needed to fight Communism whereas here, in a free country, the other danger is Catholicism of the Eastern Rite. I felt that this was very unfair to encourage people to turn away from those who did so much good for us.

Following the service, refreshments were served and I sat next to Fr. Filaret. I said to him directly and simply, 'Fr Filaret, I listened to your sermon with great attention and clearly understood that it was aimed directly at us. I want to assure you that there was no undue Catholic influence exerted on us. My husband completed the St. Nicholas Lyceum, which was run by Marion Catholic clergy. He lived there and the Lyceum educated many young poor boys and gave them an excellent education. Vova was never pressured to became Catholic. Our family, is grateful to Fr. Andrei because it is only because of him and the Catholic Church organisation behind him that we find ourself in Australia. Because of this we will never forget and will continue to nurture our close friendship. On special Feasts, especially on the Feast of St Nicholas, the Patronal Feast of their Church, we will always be there. My husband takes part in the choir and chants the Epistle but we never partake of the Sacraments.'

Fr. Filaret began to tell me that we should know about their aims and said that he will send me some books, which I have never received. Another attempt so 'protect' us was done with much more subtlety by the late Bishop Anthony, to whom I also explained our position on this matter. He understood and stopped worrying.

After Fr. Andrew was recalled to Rome, where he was enthroned as a Bishop, Fr. George Branch remained in Melbourne. We were already settled and did not require help in looking for employment but we met very often and he remains our closest friend.

The St. Nicholas Lyceum served to strongly bind these former students. Vova, together with the Sokolov and Besedin families helped Fr. George to transform a large property in Kew, Melbourne into the St. Nicholas Church and Melbourne Catholic Centre. They designed and built a chapel, which involved combining two large rooms. Walls needed to be knocked down and the balcony transformed. There were many arguments. Fr. George was worried that the roof will collapse. Vova assured him that the supporting beam will be able to hold anything, that he was sure of his calculations and practice showed that the design proved to be sturdy and effective. The chapel continued to stand

and regular services continued till Fr. George's retirement. (Following Fr. George's retirement due to ill health, the Russian Catholic Parish relocated to Caulfield where it is now called the Holy Trinity St. Nicholas Russian Catholic Parish, Melbourne and where it continues to serve the Russian speaking Catholic community to this day.)

Following our decision to send Marina to a Catholic school, Fr. George came to our home in Geelong. I remember that on that day we had a few visitors, and since our house was not large, it was impossible to find any privacy. Fr. George greeted our guests and immediately said to me, 'Galia, let us go either into your bedroom or to the car. There are too many people here and I need to speak to you seriously.'

I burst out laughing, 'What a proposition, Fr George. We better go to the car.'

He asked me directly why we decided to send Marina to a Catholic school, did we understand what could happen as a result of this decision? Were we not concerned that Marina would be taught by the Catholic nuns. He went on to mention that the strong Catholic influence could cause big problems within the family should she be drawn away from her Orthodox faith.

I really appreciated Fr. George's action. Being himself a committed Roman Catholic he chose to warn us of the strong influence of the Catholic teaching within the school and that this may become a challenge for the family. I said that I was very thankful for his words but that we took this decision seriously and felt that the strong Orthodox tradition within our family and the commitment to the faith of her parents and most importantly grandparents should provide for Marina grounding in the beliefs of their family.

'Do you realise that she may fall in love with a Catholic boy from St. Josephs College?' (This was the Catholic boys school, which was the counterpart to Sacred Heart College.)

Here I said, 'Fr. George, whatever happens will be God's will. We cannot predict what will happen in five to ten years time.'

'Remember Galina, I did warn you,' concluded Fr. George.

Marina graduated from Sacred Heart College and has warm memories of her time there. She subsequently married Basil, the son of Fr. Michael Tolmachev, Russian Orthodox priest. They had three wonderful children, Ellen, Serge and Tamara.

Basil, Marina and children - Ellen, Serge and Tamara

Fr. George's worries proved to be unfounded. Fr. Andrew Katkoff died in Rome in 1996. Fr. George continues to live in Melbourne and until very recently actively helped people and served in church. He was over 80 when he travelled to Russia and the Ukraine several times and everywhere helped the poor through gifts of money and by sending parcels. For his services to the community he was awarded a Medal by the State of Victoria in 2003 and in 2004 received the Order of Australia. People who were the recipients of his help did not forget him and nominated him for the awards. for the awards.

Russian life in Geelong was centred on church. Volodia had a marvellous baritone voice and his training at the St. Nicholas Lyceum gave him grounding in and love for church singing and the reading of the Epistle. Through his voice he adorned each church service.

There were many Russians, Ukraninans, Poles and Yugoslavs in Geelong, especially in the suburb of Bell Park. I do not know the history of this area and whether or not it was initially a park, however it was an indisputable fact that each house was surrounded by a garden with roses and many different types of beautiful flowers. There were fruit trees and many a housewife made preserves out of the bounty brought forth through our warm climate.

We had many acquaintances in Geelong but our friends lived in Melbourne and Sydney. It is unclear why this happened but the friendships were strong. We went to Melbourne often, practically each week. We went to concerts, the theatre, and visiting friends. Any excuse would do – namedays, birthdays, weddings, christenings, balls etc.

An important part of my husband's life in Geelong was volleyball. There were a number of teams, one of which was a Polish team. Once we were visiting a Polish family and Vova found out that they attended regular training and played competition volleyball. He went to a game, made a few comments and he was immediately invited to join the team, 'Syrena' and stayed with them for ten years. Later he established the Russian team 'Vostok'. He trained both the men's and women's teams and played himself. Volleyball became a very important part of his life.

When we were going though our medical examinations prior to our migration to Australia, Vova was found to have 'a sportsman's heart' which although enlarged did not translate into any symptoms or pathological signs. He felt himself to be healthy and in full strength and gave himself fully to sport. His contribution to sport in Geelong was significant so that after he passed away the sports club initiated an annual volleyball competition in his honour called, 'The Suhov Cup'. Before I subsequently remarried, I was always invited to Geelong to present the Winner's Trophy at the Suhov Cup Ball.

Having arrived in Australia, I was anxious to get a house and to create a cosy home. A car was necessary in order to move from point A to point B. The third wish was to travel to Russia and Europe. Two desires had been fulfilled. The house was fully paid for, a new car acquired so time came to travel.

Before our first trip abroad, our family suffered a terrible blow. My father became ill with throat cancer. This was a terrible disease, which took him to a better world. I loved my father very much. He was a man of strong principles, noble, honest and loyal. As mentioned, he took his pledge to remain loyal to God, the Tsar and his country very seriously. He was devoted to his family.

He enjoyed making us laugh. When asked to draw a rooster, he would start from the tail and when the pencil reached the head, the rooster became a hybrid of non-existent creatures. At this our maid Anya and I would collapse into fits of laughter.

Anya was my age. She was a fully-fledged member of our family and my close friend. She attended all my parties, accompanied me on all our picnics and went with me to the cinema. When I left to study medicine in Harbin, she missed me terribly. Later she married. When I came home for holidays I visited her but could not recognise in her the previously happy, cheeky Anya. Either her marriage was a failure or something else happened in her life – I do not know. Unfortunately, I do not even know where she went with her husband and child. Did she end up in Russia or did fate decree for her another path? Anya left a bright mark on my life.

I found it hard to cope with the death of my father, but I comforted my mother with the fact that he did not live long enough to suffer as he could have done. He died as a real Christian.

When I, with tears in my eyes said, 'Papa, why not a heart attack, why do you need to suffer?', he said, 'Galochka, this is a sign of God's mercy. He is giving me the chance to prepare for death.'

He accepted the sacrament of the Anointing of the Sick with joy and often had the sacrament of Confession and received Holy Communion.

Shortly before his death, he vehemently asked the doctors to send him home. Knowing that I was able to nurse him, the doctors allowed him to leave hospital.

He died shortly after surrounded by his family.

He blessed Marina with his own small icon of the Mother of God, an icon which remains one of her most treasured possessions. He always had a very profound influence on Marina. In an article published in the *Australiada* magazine, and later reprinted as an accompaniment to the publication of his memoirs in the Russian *Podiem Literary Journal,* Marina wrote:

Family played a huge influence on my life with the most profound being my grandfather, Ignatii Kallinnikovic Volegov. My grandfather was an officer of the White Army and remained loyal to his oath to uphold the 'Faith, the Tsar and the Fatherland' to his dying day. He was the only person who, at a reception in

China refused to drink to the health of Stalin, and managed to survive. He never justified his life's choices through hate for Russia and in spite of always remaining an anticommunist, kept his love for his beloved country and for her people. He never belonged to any organisations, which could harm Russians living in Russia, and shared her sufferings. He was open to all things new and did not fear accepting what positive changes were happening in Russia. In our house, it was never an option to hear criticism of neither the long suffering Russian Orthodox church nor any gloating on the sufferings of the Russian people.

My grandfather was brave and confident enough to apologise to a child or to shed a tear if something touched him deeply. He was open and I could speak to him about everything that was important to a child, even about The Beatles.

Following the death of my father life began to return to normal.

Marina subsequently graduated from the University of Melbourne with a Bachelor of Arts (Honours) and later completed a Diploma of Education. A year before completing her initial degree, we decided, as a gift to her, to take her overseas. When asked where she wanted to go, she replied that she wanted to meet her godfather, Lera Godoroja in Vancouver, Canada. He and his family, together with friends Rita and Kolia Vorontsov left China for Brazil five years before us, before Marina's first birthday, so her first real meeting with him was in Canada in 1972.

The meeting was touching, even after 20 years apart.

Marina at Graduation

Vova did not wish to come with us this time because it was winter in Canada. Because of university commitments before completion and the need to access the job market following graduation, it was important to remain in Melbourne during the northern warmer months. We decided to go during the Christmas holidays.

Our coming revived feelings of friendship. Kolia Vorontsov suggested, and we all agreed to meet in Russia in two years time. A cassette was recorded and sent to Vova where he was thanked for sending Marina and me to Vancouver but that in 1974 we will go to the Soviet Union. Vova and I will travel from Australia, Lera and Olia Godoroja and Rita and Kolia Vorontsov from Vancouver and that we will all meet with the Korostelev's in Lvyov. Decided – Done!

We arrived in Vancouver in time for Christmas. This is the first time that we experienced the celebration of this wonderful feast in the Western style. In China, celebrations began with the actual Feast Day of the Birth of Christ, and continued to Epiphany, we found that Christmas celebrations were in full swing. The whole city was lit up. Christmas trees were decorated and there were lights not only on the trees but houses, shops, offices were all decorated. The entire town was brights and glorious. Christmas carols emanated from all stores and the larger department stores sported big beautifully decorated Christmas trees. Long before Christmas day, which is celebrated in the West on the 25th of December, there was already a festive atmosphere.

I must confess, in spite of the fact that this tradition goes against our Orthodox tradition of having a very simple, Lenten meal featuring *kutia* (a sweet grain pudding) after the Christmas Eve church service, I enjoyed these traditional celebrations. There was a warming fire in the fireplace, the table was laden with turkey and roast with all the trimmings. There was Christmas pudding and fruitcake, an exchange of presents, Christmas music and outside there was snow. From the balcony we could see a magical city decorated with countless coloured lights and surrounded by snow capped mountains. Close to the home of the Vorontsov's was a forest. The forest itself was dark but a cascade of lights rose higher and higher up the mountain. What beauty! But most importantly, the warmth of friendship continued to warm us for many years to come.

Right up to New Year, our days were spent visiting friends, catching up and talking incessantly about our past in far away China, in Harbin and about our present lives. Our visit stirred up all memories, reignited our strong friendship and resulted in our decision to meet in Russia. We saw in the New Year with pomp and met many interesting people, many of whom we often met during future visits. Everyone was nice and kind but an old friend is so much dearer than a new one.

After all the celebrations it is with sadness that I said goodbye to Rita, Kolia, Lera and Olia and flew to San Francisco. There we also had friends and acquaintances. Again, it was time for catching up with old friends, new impressions, and new meetings. So my first trip overseas was not to Russia, as previously anticipated, but to Canada and America. So what? Marina wanted to meet her godfather and this was the correct decision because this was the first and last time that she was able to meet him. Several years later he passed due to a heart attack.

The Russian Department, where Marina studied, was established and headed by Nina Mihailovna Christesen. She started the first Russian language department in Australia. The University staged various concerts including a performance of, 'Tale of Tsar Sultan.' Australian students of the Russian language performed in this play. The director was Maria Stepanovna Stefani, who had previously shared the stage with Klavdia Shulzenko. Maria Stepanovna was a talented director and a talented singer who had a significant stage career. Marina acted as compare and performed humorous sketches. After this performance she was introduced to her future husband …

Marina and Basil were married in the Holy Trinity Serbian Orthodox Church, Nicholson Street, Melbourne. Basil's father had just been appointed as parish priest of this parish and he was due to take over those duties following the departure of Fr. Milon to London. They were married by the then Serbian Orthodox Bishop Nicholas of Australia and New Zealand, Fr. Milon, Fr. Chedomir and Fr. Michael.

The reception was at Merimu Reception Centre, Oakleigh. Guests enjoyed Russian zakuski and iced cold vodka and of course, champagne.

Marina and Basil's children - Ellen, Serge and Tamara - are now adults. They think in English, which is natural

Basil and Marina's engagement – Ludmila Tolmachev, Basil, Fr Michael Tolmachev, Antonina Volegova, Marina, Vladimir Suhov, Alexandra Suhova

since they are immersed in the language at work, with friends in daily life. They do, however, understand and speak Russian.

Some Russian traditions continue to be ingrained in them. Ellen bakes *kulichi* and makes *paskha* (Easter cheese dessert), Tamara and Serge have introduced many of their friends to the joys of Russian hospitality.

Vova and I decided to visit Russia and also go to Lvov to visit the Korostelevs. We arrived in Russia together with the Vorontsovs – Vova and I from Melbourne and Kolia and Rita Vorontsov from Vancouver. (I ask the reader's forgiveness for referring to the country as Russia. For me, it always remained 'Russia' even during Soviet occupation.)

Our entire trip proceeded together. We took all our excursions together and stayed at the Metropol Hotel in Moscow on the same floor. We also travelled to Piter (at that time many referred to Leningrad as 'Piter' or 'Peter's Place i.e. St. Petersburg), Kiev and then made our way to Lvov to visit our close friends the Korostelevs - Zenia, Valentin, Lera, their son and Valentin's father, Protodiakon Simon (Simeon Nikitich). Three men, the crux of our group, which in Harbin was called 'Kanitel', were again together.

Tears of joy, toasts, hugs, songs. Two voices, a tenor and baritone with us just trying to sing along and
then stopping in order to enjoy the men's beautiful voices. We were together for three days. During the day we took in the sights of this beautiful city and our evenings were spent around the table.

On the day of our departure there was yet again tears of joy at having met and tears of sadness at our parting. This was our first overseas trip together.

After this, we travelled a great deal. We decided to meet with the Vorontsov's every two years. Either we went to Canada or they came to Australia. We spent many wonderful hours with them travelling by car to San Fransisco, Los Angelos, San Diego, Tiuana and enjoyed some great times either exploring or just relaxing in Australia.

Endings &
New Beginnings

We got our first warning in Kiev while walking along the Shevchenko Boulevard to the Cathedral of St Vladimir.

Vova felt a tightening in his chest and needed to stop several times to catch his breath. The doctors said that he could continue his journey but he must avoid stress.

After Moscow we, together with the Vorontsovs, took a train to Brussels and then to London, Rome and Paris.

Having returned home, Vova took the advise of doctors and gave up sport, but being an avid sportsman he could not give it up immediately. He stopped playing but continued to train.

I must now tell a tragic part of our family history. It was summer 1981. Vova and I went to Sydney to attend the 50th birthday party for our friend Aliesha Belonishkin. The party went wonderfully and a few days after, a friendly game of volleyball was organised.

I went to the theatre with some friends and the men went to the volleyball. Vova played one game but decided to play another one. At the first serve, he fell. I was told later that there was great panic. They called an ambulance, took him to the hospital followed by a cortège of cars. Measures were taken but it was too late. I find it difficult to write these lines. I won't describe everything but do not want to be totally silent either.

When I needed to go through his papers at the police station, I found, in his wallet, an old and ragged envelope. Inside the envelope was a lock of my hair and my photo. Apparently, he always carried it with him.

I decided to bury Vova in Melbourne, not Geelong. Marina and her family lived in Melbourne. I decided that my place was with my family and Melbourne would be my future home.

Even now, after over 20 years it is hard to remember these difficult days. However, a person always searches for comfort and I found comfort that he died surrounded by friends, doing what he loved most – playing his favourite sport and our time in Sydney was fullof harmony and joy.

So, with the death of my husband, my life changed substantially. A move to Melbourne was imminent. I bought a house half an hour's drive from Marina and Basil's. Vova had always said that to ensure good family relations it was necessary to live close enough to be accessible when needed but far enough from each other to ensure a good relationship. I have continued to live according to this advice for many years and am happy to say that I maintain a good relationship with my daughter, son-in-law, grandchildren and the in-laws.

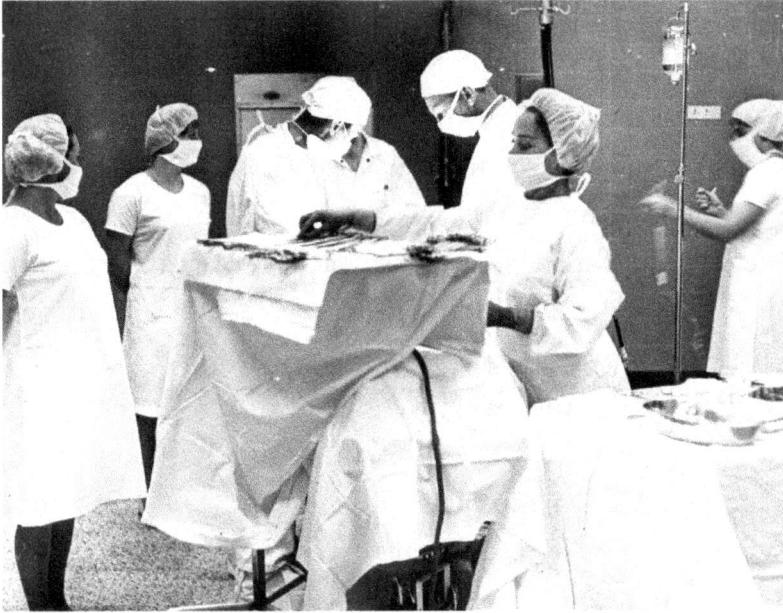

Assisting Kevin Coleman at Holy Cross Hospital
(later St John of God Hospital), Geelong

The hardest part about moving to Melbourne was leaving my beloved hospital. I had worked there for 28 years. I felt part of the hospital. I came to love my colleagues and because I organised the annual dinner dances everyone who had anything to do with Holy Cross Hospital knew me. At that time Australian workers could take long service leave. Having worked at the hospital for 25 years, I was entitled to a six month fully paid holiday. It was during that time that Vova and I went to Russia and Europe. After retuning to work for five years, I was again able to take a three month paid holiday. This proves how long I had worked at Holy Cross. It was my second home. How can I possibly leave it? How can I get up the courage to put in my resignation?

At last the day came when I decided to tell the Director of Nursing, Sister Sarto, of my decision to move to Melbourne. Sister Sarto was a kind woman who carried the weight of managing a hospital with over 200 patients. In spite of her duties she found time to appreciate God's creation, enjoy the singing of birds, to marvel at the beauty of flowers and the particular shapes of tree branches. At the same time she was exceptionally just and kind to her subordinates. Our hospital had since changed hands and was being run by a different order of nuns. It was now called, the St. John of God hospital. My decision was so very hard as my love for this hospital and my loyalty to it was great.

My last day at work was Monday and Kevin Colman had a relatively small operating list. It was sad to think that this was my last day. Even now I cannot look back on it without tears. I walk into the room where the doctors usually have their break and what do I see. The table is set. There are bottles of champagne, glasses, fruit, cakes, biscuits and all manner of nibbles. I was blown away. Such refreshments were only prepared for Christmas parties. The doctors then arrived. Flowers, presents, speeches. Kevin took it upon himself to organise, and on behalf of the surgeons presented me with an exceptionally beautiful white opal saying, 'The opal glows as brightly as did Galina in our drab, concentrated routine life.' He also said that with my happy and light personality I brought joy to himself and his colleagues. These were lovely words and I was prepared to believe that they were genuine. If I could create a lighthearted relaxed atmosphere at work then I feel that I have fulfilled my human duty.

Suddenly, hot food started to appear from the hospital kitchens. Other doctors from different hospitals started to come. Each wanted to say goodbye and to wish me good luck in Melbourne. I treasure all their presents. Each item reminds me of my second home. Everything must end and this unrepeatable day was also coming to a close.

I was soon called into the private rooms of the nuns. There, the table was also set for afternoon tea. They wanted to say goodbye to me away from other people. Warm words, prayers for my departure, presents and tears of goodbye.

Time passed. All the legalities following Vova's death were completed. The house in Melbourne was ready for a cosmetic renovation. I needed to go away, to relax and to unwind. Eight months after Vova's passing I flew to Canada. It was the correct decision. My friends heard me out, treated me with great gentleness and decided that we will not go to San Francisco where our other friends will again force me to relive what happened. We decided to go to British Colombia to enjoy the healing springs. This was such a good decision. I remain grateful to Rita and Kolia Vorontsov to this very day. Having relaxed and gained strength surrounded by those closest to me, I was able to return and to continue to cope with future difficulties.

So, the day of my departure to Melbourne came. I did not want to sell our house in Geelong because much of it was built with Vova's hands. I wanted to keep it as long as possible. I rented it and bought a very nice house with a large garden in a leafy part of Melbourne, 20 minutes from the children.

Having moved to Melbourne I continued to work in various hospitals including Bathesda. One day I noticed that I was scheduled to assist Sir. Weary Dunlop. With our gowns and masks we all tend to look the same so I was surprised when after the operation, Weary Dunlop looked for me saying, "Where is that small lady who was assisting me?" I was touched that he thanked me and began to ask me about my accent and my background. I told him that I was a Russian from China. After this I became his regular assistant. One day, my friend Olga Godoroja was visiting from Canada and we were at the opera. On seeing Sir. Dunlop among the audience, I told her about him. She said, "Galochka, if he comes up to you, I would be delighted to meet him." I said, "Come on! He will never recognize me here as he has only seen me in the operating theatre." Suddenly, I see Sir Weary Dunlop making his way towards us across the entire foyer. He told us that he had just returned from a trip to China and was very impressed with the progress made by the Chinese people in the development of their country. He not only recognized me but remembered that I had been born in China. This was not bad for a man of his age.

On the 27th of April 2005 the play, "Weary" premiered in the Atheneum Theatre in Melbourne. Naturally I could not miss it. The play was written by Alan Hopgood, directed by Roger Hogman and Weary Dunlop was played by Ronald Falk. I was shocked at he dramatic scenes played on stage and was impressed by the performance of the leading actor who captured the essence of Weary with such impeccable precision. It was difficult to comprehend that the person I was seeing on stage was not the living surgeon with whom I had the honour to work. His movements, manner, hair style, every detail created the persona of Sir Weary Dunlop. On meeting Ronald Falk after the performance, I had a chance to offer him my observations. He said that it was particularly valuable to get this kind of feedback from someone who had known the hero of the play.

At that time, wallpaper was in fashion and the house had different types of wallpaper, some dark gold, in the various rooms. I wanted more light. I hired a professional painter

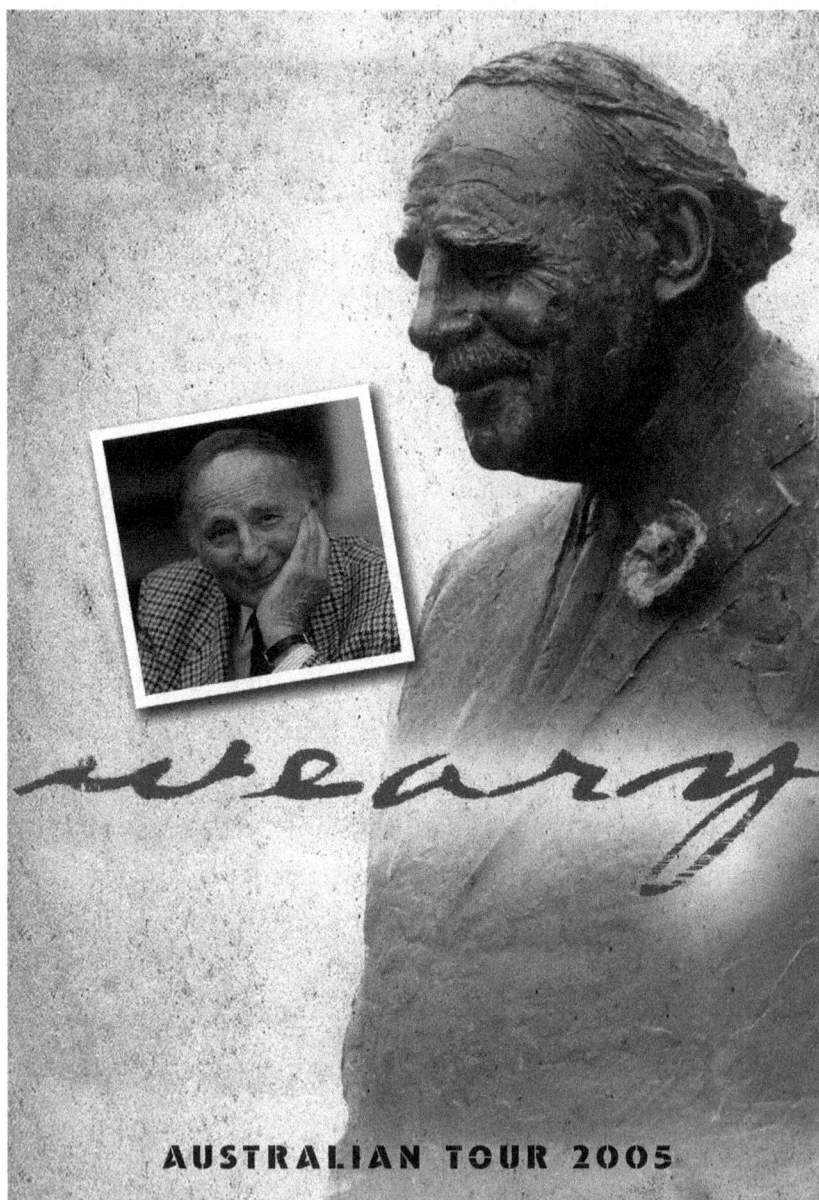

weary

AUSTRALIAN TOUR 2005

who removed the old wallpaper and I myself replaced it with beautiful silver white coloured wallpaper. The whole house became light and I was very pleased with the fact that I could cope with this difficult job by myself. It did not look bad.

My mother and I lived in this house for several years but I needed to sell it as the garden became too much to handle. The tall pine trees covered the entire yard with needles and needed to come down. This was totally beyond me so I needed to sell and to buy another similar in quality home with a small garden.

I liked the new house. It was perfect and cosy for my mother and myself. However, my mother's sister, my godmother, became ill and could not live alone. I decided to make her final years better and we decided that it would be good if she came to live with us. My mother and she would enjoy being together. She had already buried her husband, both brothers and her younger sister, who had lived with her. Now she was completely alone. Our house proved to be too small. I began to look for yet another house and immediately found a wonderful house in which some of the most remarkable events in my life took place.

We sold my godmother's house and with the sale of ours, bought this one together. I fell in love with this house as soon as I walked in. It was a very unusual and very impractical house for normal people. On one level there was a hall, two bedrooms, a bathroom and kitchen with a large stove in the middle with a big, brass, very beautiful rangehood. I placed a round table in the niche of this beautiful kitchen where we ate our meals. This part of the house was very comfortable for my mother and godmother. They had adjoining bedrooms with facilities.

My wish to provide a pleasant old age for them was made possible. They were together. They were next to each other. From the entrance hall there were eleven steps upstairs to my bedroom and study. These were two large rooms with a view onto the mountains and the sky. The study opened up onto the living room and entrance hall area. It was so lovely to look down onto the living room especially if something interesting was happening, and this happened very often.

The Australian sky is incredibly beautiful. This is not just my opinion. The Russian singer, Vika Tsiganova waxed lyrical about it when she and her husband stayed with me.

I remember a wonderful quiet evening when saying goodbye to them while standing near the house. We took a long time saying a 'Russian goodbye.'

Vika said, 'What an amazingly beautiful sky you have in Australia. It reminds me of Khabarovsk.'

It would have been tempting to spend the days staring out the window whilst sitting at my desk, but alas, there was little time. I was responsible for two, very much loved, but ill women – my mother and my godmother. At this time, they both used walkers. There were constant visits to doctors and hospitals. In our country, old people are guaranteed maximum comfort. Pensioners have deserved to have a dignified old age and they are able to access it. Medical procedures and visits to hospital are free. It is possible not to have private health insurance and still receive necessary treatment but I together with my mother and godmother had private health insurance. This gave us the ability to choose our hospitals, doctors and surgeons and if needed to be operated on immediately rather than to be on a waiting list.

For my mother this was very important because she endured three big operations. She had knee replacements on both knees and after a couple of years a total hip replacement.

'Mama!' What a short but at the same time immense word. It contains so much warmth, love, and gentleness. The love of a mother is pure, selfless and deep. Some people believe that the love of a mother is selfish because in loving her own child she revels in this feeling of love. But, even if this is so, who can possibly take away from her this wonderful feeling?

Often, during the final years of my mother's life, she would fix me with her look.

'Mama, why are you looking at me like that?' I would ask.

'I just can't get my fill gazing at you,' she would say.

Quietly, calmly, without emotion, without fervent embraces and kisses, Mama loved me with an unlimited quiet, deep and pure love.

When we came to Australia in 1957 we did not receive any government payments. On the contrary, we repaid the cost of our travel from China. Financially, we were sponsored by the World Council of Churches and we were required to pay back the cost of our travel when we gained employment.

There was plenty of work at that time. If in a family there were two working adults and a child, such as in our case, it was possible to live on one wage and to save the other one towards the purchase of a house. It was necessary to have a deposit before the bank gave a loan which needed to be repaid with a large interest. After several years, having purchased a home, savings were put into shares that eventually would bring dividends. This is how hard working people were able to buy homes and to be able to afford to travel overseas. This is how it was.

Now, my circumstances have changed. I do not need to work. Having been away from medicine for such a long time, I am far removed from the latest innovations and now use my energy in other areas which interest me.

Living in Melbourne gave me a real opportunity to meet with Russian artists who often toured Australia. There were many tours of the Moscow Circus, the Bolshoi and Kirov Ballet companies, the Symphony Orchestra featuring Svetlanov, members of the Moscow Theatre Company and various singers, musicians and comedians.

Usually I, together with some of my girlfriends, would go to a performance. After the show we would meet the artists. They were desperate for human contact and we tried to provide it for them. Usually we invited them to our homes – mostly to my home. I set the table and waited for the guests. My friends picked up the artists in several cars depending on how many artists can come. We didn't often have crowds of people although the largest reception I hosted was for soloists of the Symphoney orchestra and the Bolshoi Ballet. My friends each brought a plate and a bottle and the table was immediately laden with food. I always tried to invite my friends in order to give them the chance to meet 'the greats'.

These meetings were unforgettable. There were many get-togethers in my third house - it was ideal for these kinds of parties. There were five steps leading from the entrance hall into the living room which was large and had a big fire place above which was a brass flute. It stood on what appeared to be a stage which was perfect for performers. Beyond was a dining room and after that there was a studio with an easel, paints and bookshelves. But most interesting were the stairs from the hall to my study but overlooking the living room. During home concerts, people could view the proceedings from above and many would sit on the stairs. They could see and hear everything that was going on.

I loved this house very much. There was no better place to entertain artists. I had many famous visitors starting with Georgi Zhenov, Innokenty Smoktunovsky and Michail Zadornov. Alexandr Mallinin, Viacheslav Nevinii, Boris Sherbakov and his wife Tania, Zhenia Kindinov, Temnov, Vika Tsiganova and her husband, Bikov, Stotskii and many others.

There were also artists from the circus. Valentina Tolkunova with her brother Sergei stayed with me for several days. Svetlana Breikina stayed with me. I believe that this house admirably served its purpose. It allowed me to entertain interesting people and I continue to be friends with many of them to this day. I keep in contact with many of these people. Of course, there were some people with whom our meetings proved to be fleeting as we could not keep up contact because we were just too busy.

Marina and singer Valentina Tolkunova

Galina, Marina and actor Innokenty Smoktunovsky

Galina and humorist Michaeil Zadornov

Galina and comedian E. Shifrin

My house seemed to impress many people. It had wooden cathedral ceilings, walls and a magnificent cedar bar around which there was always a gathering of men.

Sasha Malinin arrived with his musicians. His accompanist, A. Bobrov sat at the piano and began a concert. We heard, 'Nishaia', a song that Malinin was to debut next day in public.

It is in this house that the most important family gatherings occured. I always celebrated the Name Days of my mother and godmother. On these days our family priest, Fr. Michael, served a Moleben (Prayer Service) and as a family we congratulated the person whose Name Day it was. Also, at the request of Fr. Nicholas Karipoff we held spiritual lectures/talks in this house.

My mother's death was a new tragedy, which came upon me gradually. Oh, my beautiful and loving mother.

Osteoporosis began to progress. The pain was terrible. My mother's first operation was a knee replacement. This operation went well but things did not stay that way. Her other knee needed to be operated on and this operation was also a success. After that, her hip began to deteriorate and needed to be operated on. Although the operation itself was successful, she had a bad reaction to the anaesthetic and she nearly died as a result. She stopped eating. In spite of her determination, her body activated a reflex which stopped her from swallowing food.

What do I do? I thought. *I don't know what to do.*

My mother was fading like a candle.

In this beautiful, bountiful country she was dying of starvation. But she did not want to die. She tried everything to retain the food.

'Galia,' she said to me. 'Give me a salted cucumber and I will try.'

It worked.

After the salted cucumber there came a little chicken and some bouillon. She began eating small portions of food and gaining weight. Just as my mother started to feel better, another tragedy ...

My godmother was living alone at the time, about 45 minutes drive from my home. I went to visit her, only to find her sitting close to tears. She sitting on her chair, unable to move because of the terrible pain in her knees. It was impossible to leave her alone like this. I packed her bags and took her to my home. An unforgettable meeting occurred here, in the family room.

The family room was off the kitchen area. It was the place where my mother and I would sit and watch TV, where visiting children could be entertained. This was like a family living room that enabled the homemaker to be part of the family even while she was busy cooking in the kitchen. I had two identical recliners with a small coffee table in between. After work in the evening I would often join my mother here and enjoy a cup of tea while watching TV.

I sat my godmother down on one of the chairs in the family room. She did not want to eat and refused everything I offered to her. I calmed her down, rang my doctor and arranged an appointment for the next day.

Since it was a Sunday, I brought out a silver tray with two shots of vodka, a salted cucumber and some salted herring. My godmother was affronted saying that she does not drink. But my mother understood the situation and quietly said to her, 'Drink Marussia, take a bite of the cucumber.'

My godmother was by nature a strong woman who was used to being in control. However, she listened to my mother

The next day I took my godmother to my doctor and began her medical treatment. She soon began walking again. The experiment with the silver tray with the vodka and the herring was not repeated but the sisters began to live peacefully and relatively happily, together. Their respective health problems, although continuing to be painful, were alleviated somewhat with targeted medical treatments. This showed that my godmother could not live alone in her house. However, it was impossible to put her with all her belongings into only one room in my house. I decided to sell her house and my house and to buy a house together.

When my mother needed a full hip replacement the surgeon was aware that there could be complications due to her age and fully explained what her life will be like if she did not have an operation. She would need to be totally bed bound and gradual decline towards death. He was anxious that I should make the correct decision so that I would never blame myself for making an incorrect one. What he did not realise was that my mother had a bright mind and that she was able to decide for herself.

She decided, 'Galina, invite Fr. Michael so that he can give me the sacrament of the Anointing of the Sick and then I will make my decision.'

She bravely sat through the entire service, prayed and

only then asked that an ambulance be called. They took her to the hospital and again followed painful tests, x-rays, moves in and out of bed and into wheelchairs with each movement being accompanied by extreme pain because of her broken hip. At last – the operation with all its expected complications. The situation was critical. There was little hope of recovery. But, oh how she wanted to live!

Fr. Nicholas Karipoff, having visited her and hearing her confession said to me, 'You know, she does not want to die.'

I knew that. She had a happy life, with a loving husband. She loved me unconditionally. She had a granddaughter, Basil, grandchildren and she felt their love and respect.

In our family my mother was the matriarch, not a tyrant, but a respected anchor, a beloved matriarch. She fought each moment for her life. Just before the operation my mother recorded her life story onto two cassettes. She spoke of her family in Miass. She remembered all the names and it is with this information that I subsequently went to Miass in 2000. I have written about this and subsequent visits in my Travel Journals of 2000, 2001 and 2003.

My mother died on the 22nd of December 1991. I survived the loss of my beloved father, my husband but the loss of my mother remains with me to this very day. To see her unceasing suffering over a period of two months and feeling helpless was unendurable.

Marina and Basil decided that I needed to go somewhere to have a change of atmosphere. Decided – done.

One day, during a family celebration some members of

the family rand a distant relative in Paris , who was once a actress, Zoya Valevskaya telling her that I am going to Paris. I was stunned but quickly got my bearings. I was sent to Paris and Zoya and I visited Monte Carlo where we spent two weeks. I managed to fly to Moscow from Paris.

Galina and friends at home in Melbourne

All this happened in 1992. I was in Paris for my birthday and my Name Day. To celebrate, some of my favourite friends came to visit me, friends whom I previously entertained in my own home, G. Zhenov with his wife Lidia Petrovna, Artem, now Professor Rudnitski, Zenia Kindinov, I. Smoktunnovsky with his daughter, Masha. I returned from Moscow to Paris and then home. There, another tragedy awaited me ...

The health of my godmother worsened dramatically. She

became very suspicious, difficult and aggressive. I thought that this was because of her personality because she was always the strong one in the family. Together with her very ill husband, Roman Petrovich Protodiakonov, two brothers and a sister lived with her. She cared for them all and eventually buried them. However, she was suffering from a progressive illness which was affecting her personality. Life was hard. It is hurtful to bear the brunt of unfounded accusations, but God was merciful to me.

One wonderful morning, one that I will never forged, she was waiting for me at the foot of the stairs. I came down from my bedroom and she greeted me with a smile, something I had not seen in a long time.

'Galina, will you take me to church?' she asked.

I could not believe my ears. She has been categorically refusing to go anywhere at all even to church. Today I was seeing before me my loving godmother of old and she was even asking my advice on what she should wear, what blouse, which shoes etc We went to church.

After that, life continued in a normal and quiet fashion. Love again resurfaced in our home. But this was not to last long. My godmother suffered that which she had always feared most. She became paralysed. The stroke chained her to her bed for the next two years. Her condition did not improve and she eventually passed away in the St. John of Khronsdadt, Russian Aged Care facility.

I was left completely alone in the large house which was showing signs of wear and tear. I decided to look for something more appropriate but during this period of searching for a new home, Vadim Kuchin came into my life. He came from Sydney, but not as a knight in shining armour on a white horse, but in a red car. He introduced himself and as I later found out, decided his fate.

Vadim was slightly older than me, a widower. After a long illness, his wife died, leaving him with two married sons and six grandchildren.

Vadim, an engineer, was originally from Harbin. All my old Harbin and Sydney friends knew him as an honest and good person. This was a great reference, however, I was noncommittal.

Vadim turned out to be very determined and asked permission to visit me on the following weekend. This time he came by plane. Everything happened with lightening speed.

Masha, the friend who introduced us, prepared a full speech, 'Be aware that he is a wonderful person. Do not scare him with your bohemian lifestyle. He had a very shy wife and they led a very quiet and secluded life.'

How could I not scare him with my bohemian lifestyle when on the first night of his arrival I was visited by Alexander Malinin with two of his musicians? Naturally, I invited all my friends, as was usual when entertaining celebrities. They all brought a plate, the table was set and this happened to also be the birthday of Sasha Malinin. Feasting, music, singing. As I mentioned before, he sang 'Nishei', a song that he was due to premier at his concert the next day.

Galina, and Vadim

I invited all my single girlfriends to this party. There were four of them and I was the fifth. Vadim had many to choose from. But, he had already made his choice at our first meeting.

And so my daughter and her family welcomed Vadim into the family.

We had mutual friends living in Melbourne because he also studied at the Harbin Polytechnic Institute. My fate was decided. He proposed to me. My aunt, Lidia Ivanovna Antonova, was charmed by him and advised me to accept his proposal.

The wedding was very family oriented. Aunt Lidia blessed me and my nephew and godson, Alex Vinogradov escorted me to church. Vera, his mother, and my cousin, was my *svaha* (match-matcher) and Masha Belonojkina, who introduced us, was Vadim's *svaha*. Now taking on the role of maid of honour was Masha Belonijkina, who introduced us. But the most beautiful decorations at our wedding were our grandchildren who acted as our attendants. Vadim had six grandchildren and I – three. The girls wore dresses made of a delicate material with a pink floral design. They had pink flowers in their hair. The boys were in black pants, white shirts and pink bow ties.

Two priests married us, my son-in-law's father, Fr. Michael and Fr. Peter. The reception was in my home. The house was decorated with tea pink roses and carnations with garlands flowing down the staircase beautifully done by Natasha Nikolaeff.

We had 75 guests. It would have been impossible to seat everybody so caterers served finger food and champagne, together with other drinks, on large silver trays. However, the men preferred to gather around the bar, a fixture of the house which we still remember to this day. It was so beautiful and many interesting and warm times were enjoyed around it.

Naturally, we could not have a celebration without a concert. After the official speeches and toasts, Sergei Suetin played, 'Amur Waves' and we 'opened the ball' with a short dance. Then followed soloists, Sonia Bantos, Fred and Raia Burstain, Svetlana Chernavina, an impromptu choir and the festivities continued well into the night.

Masha and Alesha Belonojkin came from Sydney and Olga Godoroja from Canada.

Galina and Vadim's wedding day

Having flung the bouquet, Vadim and I left our house guests to fend for themselves at home and left to spend the night at the beautiful historic Windsor Hotel. Unfortunately, no one caught the wedding bouquet which by Australian tradition would have meant that the person who was lucky enough to catch it would marry next.

It is difficult to believe that over ten years have passed from that marvellous day. I had lived with my first husband for 30 years. In fact, he died just two weeks short of our 30th wedding anniversary.

I have been fortunate enough to establish a very good relationship with my two stepsons, Vadmin's sons, Vadim and Alex. Vadim has a good relationship with Marina.

Cultural Life –
Russian Theatrical Society
& the Solouhin Literary Society

While I have written about my family life and hospital work, I'm yet to touch on my stage and literary life ...

Once a year, the Russian language newspaper *Edinenie* (Unification) organised a big ball. The ball was always grand and the atmosphere was usually festive. It was a black tie event and everyone went to great effort to look glamorous. There was music, dancing a wonderful meal.

At that time, there were strict licensing laws and because of this people needed to bring alcoholic drinks as the venue was not allowed to sell them. To an extent seeing beautifully dressed people carrying in eskys or brown paper bags of alcohol ruined the atmosphere of the ball, but once the bottles of champagne, spirits and wine were put on the tables, the ball regained an atmosphere of festive style.

After one of those balls, we were invited by close friends

to a birthday celebration. The table was set with light *zakuski (entrées)* and there were many bottles of champagne cooling in a bath of ice.

During that period of my life, whenever I would see a bottle of champagne, I would start to feel tipsy. As soon as the bottle cork hit the roof, I was already drunk. I was genuinely happy and joyous.

I remember how we partied. We danced and sang until morning. We did not plan to drive back to Geelong and planned to stay at Fr. George's.

In the morning I received a phone call from the well-mannered voice of Sasha Ilyin.

'Galina Ignatievna, I am sorry to bother you. I rang your home but your mother told me that you were in Melbourne, at Fr. George's. I am happy to have found you. The thing is that as group of friends, we have many talented people who sing and dance among us. We decided to combine our talents and perform on stage. This way we will be able to start to give a love for Russian culture to our children. We have prepared a concert and hope that you will agree to compare it.'

I categorically refused saying that I have never been on stage, that I was not an actress. He gently reminded me that he did see me in the role of compare at the concert of Karasev and can even prove this with photographs. Yes, this really happened and I had forgotten about it.!

A well-known dancer, Karasev, brought his company to Geelong. The night before the concert I was asked to

Galina on stage with the Russian Theatrical Society

compare it. I could not refuse and as there was no time for rehearsal, I was given a list of dances and performers and just needed to introduce the acts. This was so primitive that I managed to forget about it. However, Sasha remembered and decided that only I would be suitable for the role. I did suggest that he consider other, younger women for the role, but he was adamant that he wanted me to do it. My head was thumping from the wild night before, so I was not strong enough to refuse and asked Sasha to ring me at home in the evening. He agreed.

The day of the concert arrived. The performers were definitely talented. Sasha Ilyin, who was also its choreographer and dancer, directed the dance group which was the main feature of the concert. There was also a choir, a string orchestra, a reading by Sonia Bantos and dramatic sketches.

Sonia and Vladimir Brjosovsky were the soloists. They sang to the accompaniment of the string orchestra. In fact, this was the start of concerts, which continued to be bright, and of a very professional level.

In preparing for the first concert, Sasha gave me full freedom to choose my material. He only asked me to include an explanation of the aims of the 'Russian Theatrical Society.' The aim was to introduce our children to Russian culture, and to develop in them a love for Russian song, Russian dance and most importantly, the Russian language.

At this time, in 1974, we were reading Solzhenitsin. For my

performance I chose a short Solzhenitsin, 'The Duckling'. I loved this story so much and in future read all these small stories on stage. However, 'The Duckling' was my first. I read a comedy piece about a man tackling housework using new equipment. I introduced the dances and filled in during the various changes of scenery. I must say that this experience gave me the confidence to go on stage.

As each self-respecting woman, my first thought was about what dress I will wear on stage. I took three dresses out of my cupboard but was not able to choose so I put all three into the car.

Arriving in the theatre, I was asked to check the microphone and lights. With a microphone in my hand, I was amazed that my voice could be heard. Once the lights were directed at me, I was hooked. I felt the magic of the stage. I will be heard, I will be seen and I stopped worrying. After that, I turned my attention to my wardrobe and tried to to decide which dress to wear.

'All three,' said a lady who was passing by.

'What do you mean, all three? I am not a prima-donna, I am only a compare.'

The lady said that the public will be bored with seeing just one dress and would like to see the compare in different outfits.

I was happy with this advice and decided to change with each part of the concert. I saw my cousin, a boy of 13, who was part of the string orchestra.

'You look nice!' he said.

We all know that children tell the truth and I accepted the compliment. This gave me more confidence and I went out onto the stage fully confident that I am seen and heard. I enjoyed myself tremendously.

After that first concert, I continued to work with the company for the next ten years till the Russian Theatrical Society came under the directorship of L. Bakseeva, who removed from the Society everything other than the dances. The main aim of the Theatrical Society was killed and it became just a dance company.

To this very day I remain grateful to Sasha Ilyn that he saw something in me, which I did not even recognise in myself and through which he managed to open a new page in my book of life. Thank you, Sasha.

Years passed. Many things changed in my life. The death of my husband, the loss of my much loved mother, my second marriage.

Somehow I began to organise the traditional Days of Russian Culture. My first year in this role found me in a panic because talented people were reaching a time in their lives when performing was getting more and more difficult for them. Some were leaving the theatre stage, others were leaving this world stage altogether.

I began to collect performers from our die hards and from the newly arrived people from Russia. I collected many artists. No one refused. When I realised that there was no way that we will fit into two hours, I did not have the nerve to turn anyone away because I was afraid to offend people. As a result, the concert lasted for four and a half hours. This was an unforgettable concert because of its duration and content. Performers included soloists, Tania Stoyanova, Lena Yashenko, Ivan Bogut, Polina Volsoini and dramatic actors – Maya Menglet, Leonid Satanovsky, Anna Larionova. The string orchestra, 'Sadko' and the dance group also performed. But four and a half hours was too much and people remembered this concert for many years to come. I also did not forget this concert. From then on I always made sure that I kept a time limit on 'Days of Russian Culture.'

In the same way, unbeknown to me, I became the founder of the Solouhin Literary Society. Professor G.A. Tvetov came to Sydney on the invitation of G.P. Logunov. During a radio interview given by the professor, I heard about V. Solouhin for the first time. I was interested in his presentation and made sure that I missed neither his talks, nor the articles published in *Edinenie*. His articles and talks were about the rural or country literary movement. At the initiative of my acquaintance, A. Perina, we invited Professor Tsvetov to Melbourne and arranged a talk in the home or Fr. George. Here he introduced us to the works of the 'country literary writers'.

Personally, my interest in V. Solouhin began in the '70s, when I read *Black Boards*. After that, I came across a small brochure, *Reading Lenin,* published outside the Soviet Union. I was amazed. It summarised what had been

Galina on stage at 'Days of Russian Culture'

previously written by Lenin and had gone unnoticed. Such horror was included in these words, such a terrible sentence passed onto an unsuspecting innocent people. The intelligencia, clergy and peasantry – all suffered the consequences of such a draconian policies.

I developed an amazing respect for Solouhin. I began to acquaint myself with his poems, prose and decided to establish a literary society. I was immediately supported by friends and with their help, on the first anniversary of the death of the poet and writer we served a *Panikhida* (Memorial Service) at the Cathedral of the Protecting Veil, Melbourne, and following this, in the church hall, had the inaugural meeting of the V. Solouhin Russian Literary Society. Professor G.A. Tsvetov sent us a videocassette of the life of Solouhin. His poems were recited.

The people at this first meeting were A. Eksarkho, V. Kosse, O.Shonina, S. Suetin, G. Nekrasov, A. Karel, I. Smolianinov and myself. These are the people who began this group. I was elected its President and continue to work in this role to this day. We meet once a month. The topic of discussion is decided upon by members according to their specific interests or in answer to specific requests from the public. Since literature is so closely associated with theatre, I suggested that our organisation join with the Russian Theatrical Society and be renamed, 'The Soluhin Literary and Theatrical Society'. This suggestion was upheld by everyone and now exists under the auspices of the Russian Ethnic Representative Council of the state of Victoria.

We hold monthly lectures and every two to three months I organise chamber concerts in the hall of Russian House. The Day of Russian Culture concerts were dedicated to a writer or composer or a special day. The concerts are usually held in Melba Hall, University of Melbourne.

I am happy that my efforts give people the pleasure of hearing such brilliant minds as Fr. Igor Filianovsky, who continues to be a constant source of knowledge in the field of literature and theology.

Professor O. Donskih conducted a full cycle of lectures on literature and history. Nina Makarova, art historian, presented a series of lectures on Art Appreciation. G.M. Nekrasov, author of many books, gave many lectures and members of the Union of Writers, A.M. Karel and I.M. Smolianinov, gave presentations and poetry readings.

Fr. Igor Filianovsky

A young bard, Michael Yarovoi, prepared an interesting lecture on Maxmillian Voloshin. Olga Shonina gave many presentations, as did Sergei Suetin and many others.

At present I am preparing a Day of Russian Culture concert dedicated to Glinka and Chehov.

In drawing conclusions about my life, I clearly understood that each period of one's life carries with it special joys and difficulties. It is difficult to say which period of my life was, for me, the happiest. However, I can definitely say that the period that is the calmest and most creative is definitely the time of maturity.

Life experience, gained over many years, gives a feeling of confidence and accomplishment. What richness has been accumulated over a long life!

For me, the most precious things in life are people, and I am immeasurably rich. My dear loving and loved family, friends, acquaintances and all people whom I met along life's path have enriched my existence – making it interesting, fulfilling and meaningful.

I cannot stop being grateful to God for His generous gift.

Galina and Fr. Igor Filianovsky giving a lecture during the Solouhin society meeting.

Epilogue

Seven years passed after I put the final full stop at the end of my memoir. Life continues, world events unfold with amazing swiftness and do not pass by us, without leaving their mark on the fate of mankind. I won't write about global events, or the incredibly complex political situation placing individuals on different sides of the barricades. I will confine myself to our small family.

During this time, great sadness came to me. Vadim Kuchin, my husband, died from heart disease in September 2005. His sons, Vadim and Alexander, together with their families, were with me during this time. They were irreplaceable in their support and remain to this day close and dear to me.

My daughter, Marina and her husband Basil are my strength. Following discussions about how I should organise my life after the death of Vadim, I decided to accept the invitation of my children to build a house on their property. It was not realistic to stay alone in a big house. I approached the new project with my natural enthusiasm and the task was accomplished rather quickly. The most pressing difficulty was to move from a large house to a relatively small one. I needed to dispose of large pieces of furniture, and was able to give up certain household goods. However, it proved impossible to liquidate books from my library, paintings and other much loved things. I created my own world in the new house and attained total happiness living next to my daughter and son-in-law. I do not miss my old house, although can admit to a slight tinge of sadness when I drive past it. But this is all in the past. Now, I live fully in the present.

Many happy events have occurred in the family. Ellen, my granddaughter, the one who accompanied me to Russia in 2001, married Gino Vigilante and presented her husband with two gorgeous girls, Amelia Lucia and Gianna Antonia as well as a son, Edward Michael.

Serge, the middle child of the Tolmachev family, married Heather Miller. They have two children – Adam Michael and Lila Sophia. Their third child, Tamara has not met the hero of her dreams but seems not in too much of a hurry to do so. I call her Tamara 'Prekrasnaia' because she is actually a very beautiful young woman both physically and within her soul and is also very wise.

All my grandchildren are very friendly towards each other and meet regularly. They are also close to Vadim's grandchildren. Unfortunately, we rarely see Vadim's oldest grandson, Nicholas, because he lives in Hong Kong with his wife, Wendy. But we do catch up with Paul and Erica, the children of Vadim and Bronwyn and Bridget, Natalie and Michael, the children of Alex and Kerry. Erica and her husband Jamie Kendrick have one son – Rhys Douglas and Natalie and her fiancée, Jonathan Willams have two lovely daughters, Katja and Ruby with Levi, a son, in the middle.

Sadly my stepson, Vadim Kuchin, passed away on the 28th of August 2015. Although he had been ill for quite some time, he died a much loved and respected man.

From the Kuchin family I now go to the family of Basil's sister, Maria. She married Michael Radze and they had two children – Zoe and Andrew. Both are married. Zoe married Alasdair Brooks and Andrew married Jane Edwards. Andrew and Jane have a girl, Sasha, and boy, Sam. All three branches form the basis of the youngest generation of our family.

There were also many changes in my life. Having such a wide circle of friends from the world of the arts – actors, musicians, singers and generally talented and interesting people I was propelled into a frantic social life. My house was always open for gatherings, premiers, concerts, parties and meetings with visiting Russian celebrities who as part of their tour found themselves 'performing' at my place. I always invited my friends in order to give them the opportunity to rub shoulders with the likes of Smoktunovsky, Zsenov, Zadornov, Malinin, Tolkuniv and many others. Now, in modern Russia, such famous people are in great demand and are not available to us any more.

I also continued to develop the Solouhin Literary and Theatrical Society and organised the annual 'Day of Russian Culture' as well as other concerts and presentations. On the 12th of June 2013 I put on a big concert in honour of the Day of Russia. Participants included Anatoli Dokumentov (Honoured Artist of Russia), the Melancholy Trio featuring O. Vakusevich, V. Yrgaevai and V. Bilogan. Also performing were students of the Susan Thomson Russian Choreographic Academy. Russian teachers, Maxim and Yulia Vasilev presented a compilation of Russian folk, the waltz from Tchaikovsky's ballet, 'Sleeping Beauty' and the Spanish dance from L. Minkus's ballet, 'Don Quixote'. The public was in raptures over the performance of Anastasia Korolev on percussion. Her rendition of Rimsky Korsikov's, 'Flight of the Bumble Bee' and the 'Italian Polka' by S. Rachmaninov. There was also a string quartet. V. Fedorovskaya gave a superb rendition of, 'I Love You Russia' and 'Russian Evenings, Full of Rapture.' Alexander Vengerovski (Honoured Artist of Russia) and Larissa Hranovskaia created a truly Russian atmosphere with their performance of Russian folk songs.

I have always tried to encourage Russian culture within the Australian context and featured the superb bass, Anthony Mackay, singing Gremin's aria from the opera 'Eugene Onegin' by P. Tchaikovsky, the aria of Dosifei from the opera 'Havanchin' by Muzorski as well as songs from the 'Suite' by D. Shostakovich. The compare, Ludmilla

Ruban, handled her difficult task with dignity.

This was my final concert. I have written a great deal about the cultural life of Melbourne in the Australian journal, 'Australiada' and 'Rodnaya Ladoga' and 'Sibir', published in St Petersburg and Irkutsk.

After many years I decided to pass the baton to the younger generation. I called a committee meeting of the Solouhin Society and passed the presidency of the organisation to Olga Shonina, who had been in at the start of the society in the role of Secretary. I wish her the committee many successes and am certain that she will be effective in her role.

I remain an honorary member of the Society. I have now transferred by efforts to writing. I write stories and articles for *Australiada* and *Edinenie*, published in Australia and continue to be published in Russia through Rodnaya Ladoga and Sibir. My book, *People And Their Destiny Through Letters* was published by Nestor-Istoria, St. Petersburg. We held book launched in Sydney and Melbourne.

Some books remained in Russia and others sent to the United States. I am getting very positive feedback from readers, which is very gratifying.

In conclusion I would like to say that my stormy life which was full of work with exceptionally interesting and talented people is reflected in my books. Writing my books enabled me to relive my life, the remember the feelings of happiness and sadness, to remember my relationships with

Galina's book launch, Melbourne

people, the letters that I have received and at the same time to introduce the reader to the extraordinary people I have met.

Now, in my cosy home, close to my family I gain pleasure from my great grandchildren, from their children's chatter, from their laughter. All things are normal. Dances and home concerts remain in one's memory and in various recordings. But I must say that my credo is to remember the past, live in the present with the hope of a kind and bright future. I hope that I have fulfilled my duty to those people close to me and now accept a new role of peace, reflection and thankfulness to the life that God has so generously given me. However, I am not one to completely stop creating and I want to finish the novel, *Between Two Worlds*, which I started many years ago. It would also be nice to try my hand at painting again.

Galina Kuchina (nee Suhova and Volegova)
31 October 2015

Memoirs
of *Galina*

GALINA KUCHINA

ISBN 9781925367225   Qty

RRP   AU$24.99   .....

Postage within Australia   AU$5.00   .....

TOTAL* $_____

* All prices include GST

Name:...

Address: ....

....

Phone:...

Email: ....

Payment: ❑ Money Order ❑ Cheque ❑ MasterCard ❑ Visa

Cardholder's Name:...

Credit Card Number: ....

Signature:..

Expiry Date: ....

Allow 7 days for delivery.

Payment to: Marzocco Consultancy (ABN 14 067 257 390)
PO Box 12544
A'Beckett Street, Melbourne, 8006
Victoria, Australia
admin@brolgapublishing.com.au

BE PUBLISHED

Publish through a successful publisher.
Brolga Publishing is represented through:
• **National** book trade distribution, including sales,
marketing & distribution through **Macmillan Australia.**
• **International** book trade distribution to
    • The United Kingdom
    • North America
    • Sales representation in South East Asia
• **Worldwide e-Book distribution**

For details and inquiries, contact:
Brolga Publishing Pty Ltd
PO Box 12544
A'Beckett St VIC 8006

Phone: 0414 608 494
markzocchi@brolgapublishing.com.au
ABN: 46 063 962 443
(Email for a catalogue request)

www.ingramcontent.com/pod-product-compliance
Lightning Source LLC
Chambersburg PA
CBHW062051270326
41931CB00013B/3022